Battleg

VERDUN–FC   [

Christina Holstein

Series Editor
Nigel Cave

Pen & Sword
MILITARY

First published in Great Britain in 2002
reprinted 2010 by
Pen & Sword Military
an imprint of
Pen & Sword Books Ltd
47 Church Street
Barnsley
South Yorkshire
S70 2AS

ISBN 978 1 84884 345 5

Typeset in 10pt Times
Printed and bound by CPI UK

Pen & Sword Books Ltd incorporates the Imprints of Pen & Sword
Aviation, Pen & Sword Maritime, Pen & Sword Military, Wharncliffe
Local History, Pen and Sword Select, Pen and Sword Military
Classics, Leo Cooper, Remember When, Seaforth Publishing and
Frontline Publishing.

For a complete list of Pen & Sword titles please contact
PEN & SWORD BOOKS LIMITED
47 Church Street, Barnsley, South Yorkshire, S70 2AS, England
E-mail: enquiries@pen-and-sword.co.uk
Website: www.pen-and-sword.co.uk

Battleground Europe

VERDUN

FORT DOUAUMONT

Battleground series:

CONTENTS

A captured
German
maxim in Fort
Douaumont.

Introduction by Series Editor

Verdun is the name above all that the French - and probably the Germans - associate with the carnage and human loss that was the First World War. The battle near this ancient and historically important town was the longest in the war, although the casualties endured there were substantially less than those on the Somme in the same year and on a par with those at Third Ypres, better known as Passchendaele. The policy of the French army of rotating divisions through the battle arena ensured that a large proportion of the French army endured the unimaginable torment of a stint in the line there; whilst the area involved in the fighting was much less than, for example, on the Somme.

The visitor to Verdun will find a battlefield that is not easy to 'read'. The post war forestation programme makes viewing the battle site difficult. On the other hand there is plenty that remains on the ground, and undoubtedly the most emotive part of that 'sacred soil' is Fort Douaumont.

For some time now I have been looking for someone to write guides to Verdun: someone who could manage to write in English and yet read the sources in French and German. Christina Holstein has surpassed all my hopes, producing an outstanding and meticulously researched guide. Until now, certainly, it has been possible to visit Douaumont, and there has been a self-guided tour available in English. But the detail of the tour provided here - not least by the lucid technical explanations of everything from the way in which the guns worked to the construction methods used in the fort - will bring a whole new level of understanding to the visitor. The bonus is that the story of the fort has been put firmly into its context and has been accompanied by graphic accounts of the men who fought here.

The result of this labour is probably the finest guide in any language to this part of Verdun. I look forward with real anticipation to future works by Christina Holstein on Verdun in the years to come. From the point of view of the series as a whole, it is also a great pleasure to be able to write the introduction to the first book we have done which covers the effort of the French army. For various reasons this has been a big gap in the British knowledge of the war, and this guide is an excellent start to try and correct the balance. And, of course, it throws further light on that formidable fighting machine, the German army.

One cannot read this book without wondering at the endurance of the human spirit.

Nigel Cave, *Casta Natale, Rovereto.*

The tattered flags of a French Division are being paraded in honour of French soldiers who fought at Verdun. General Gouraud, who lost an arm in the war, is standing on the right.

AUTHOR'S NOTE

In telling the story of the battle for Fort Douaumont I have tried to make equal use of French and German sources. In doing so, I have met the sort of difficulties that one always meets when trying to match opposing views of the same event. In this case they are compounded by recollections written years later, maps drawn earlier than the events that they record, and texts which – through translation and re-translation – have departed from the original. To take just a few examples, I have scratched my head long and hard over the reconciliation – ultimately impossible – of the differing outlines on French and German maps of the vital forested areas of Hassoule Wood, La Vauche Wood and Hermitage Wood, which were the scene of great events on the afternoon of 25 February 1916. Accounts of the German infantry attack on Fort Douaumont on that day speak variously of heavy snow, a few flakes or no snow at all. Different reports of the French capture of the acting German commandant of Fort Douaumont in October 1916 – by one or more French soldiers from the same or different regiments – place him in the middle of the main ground floor corridor of the barracks, sitting on the bed in his quarters on the lower floor, or burning papers in the fire raging in the pioneer depot. As if this were not enough, the translation of texts between French and German can result in important features of the fort taking on a series of aliases that can be difficult to untangle. The main ground floor corridor in the barracks has at least five different names in German, to say nothing of the French versions of the same thing. To make matters worse, authors who quote from one another re-translate the terms into a further series of headaches for the researcher, sometimes creating, as they do so, an entirely new feature which actually did not exist. The crowning problem, though, is the time. German time, which was normally one hour ahead of French time, was two hours ahead during the unsuccessful French attempt to retake Fort Douaumont in May 1916. The difficulties of trying to reconcile French and German accounts of attack and counterattack on and around the fort between 22 May and 24 May 1916, using sources that may or may not be aware of the difference and which quote from each other without making allowance for it, are too trying for this author to recall.

I have tried my best to make sense of all this and, in doing so, the empty fort has come to life. I hope that the men, both French and German, who knew it during the dark days of 1916 will recognize my story and will forgive any errors that I might have made.

INTRODUCTION

On 13 July 1936, 15,000 veterans of the First World War gathered in front of the Douaumont Ossuary at Verdun to swear an oath of peace and to observe one minute's silence. Among the 500 strong German delegation was former *Oberleutnant* Cordt von Brandis, one of two officers who had been awarded the *Pour le Mérite*, Germany's highest decoration, following the capture of Fort Douaumont on 25 February 1916. Von Brandis – whose role in the capture of Fort Douaumont was not quite as important as he had successfully managed to portray - had became a national hero, a favourite with the Crown Prince of Germany, a best selling author and had even had a village in Prussia named after him. The captors of other forts had not fared so well. What was special about Fort Douaumont?

A visitor only has to walk up on to the shell torn top of the fort to start to see why it is different. At 395 metres above sea level, Fort Douaumont is the highest point on the battlefield of Verdun and from its summit one can easily see why it was placed there. It dominates everything. All around, it offers wide views of the sort commanders dream of and which are not found elsewhere within a radius of fifteen

Aerial view of Fort Douaumont in 2001. Jean-Luc Kaluzko

Post-war view of Fort Douaumont.

miles. In 1914 twenty eight major and intermediary forts formed a double ring around the city of Verdun but it was Fort Douaumont which was the cornerstone of the system. Repeatedly modernized from 1887 onwards, strengthened with a thick layer of special concrete and heavily armed, it was, in General Pétain's words, 'the key to the battlefield'. The Germans could hardly believe their luck when on 25 February 1916, four days into the Battle of Verdun, it fell almost undefended into their hands.

Ninety four years after the Battle of Verdun, the virtual abandonment of Fort Douaumont by the French and its almost accidental capture by a handful of German soldiers are no less astonishing than they were then. Possession of the fort not only gave the Germans an incomparable observatory, front line depot and barracks but it strengthened their morale as much as it demoralized the French. In the words of one French general, the loss of Fort Douaumont was as much of a blow to the French army as the whole of the first four days of the battle, which saw the destruction of an army corps and the loss of masses of artillery. Morale and national pride, quite as much as its dominating position, demanded that Fort Douaumont be recaptured.

The Crown Prince of Germany wrote in his memoirs that when the fort was captured, the Germans were 'within a stone's throw of victory'. But he had no reserves with which to follow up the early successes and the crucial moment passed. As the months ground on without significant success on either side, Fort Douaumont became the heart of the battle. For each side, the desire to keep it or to recapture it became itself the reason to go on fighting. One French historian of the battle states that the loss of Fort Douaumont caused the French over 100,000 casualties. How many lives would have been saved on both sides if,

Shell damage to the south side of the barracks.

when the battle began, it had been properly garrisoned and armed?

During the months that followed its fall and despite a bombardment of unprecedented length and ferocity, the fort did – for the Germans, at least - what it was supposed to do; it formed a strongpoint and a centre of resistance. Its concrete carapace was laid bare by the furious bombardment but it held. Despite poor ventilation, primitive hygiene, a major explosion and several fires the fort continued to offer shelter, food, rest and basic medical facilities to thousands of men. While life inside was not comfortable, it was better than the indescribable horror in the belt of fire that surrounded it. Once recaptured on 24 October 1916, Fort Douaumont was repaired and finally used for its intended purpose: to support the French infantry in their efforts to drive the Germans back.

The role of Fort Douaumont did not come to an end with its recapture in October 1916, nor even with the Armistice in 1918. The fort taught the French two lessons: first, that forts alone could not stop the enemy but, second, that they increased the means of resistance of troops who knew how to make use of them. After the war, French military engineers studied the strengths and weaknesses of Fort Douaumont and used their findings in the design of the Maginot Line. As a result, during the 1920s and 1930s, France once again put her faith in the defensive capabilities of steel and concrete. But by the time war came again, close co-operation between aircraft and swiftly moving armoured fighting vehicles had swung the pendulum back in favour of the offensive.

From most parts of the battlefield, Fort Douaumont is today hidden from view by a thick forest which largely hides the scars of battle. A

11

visitor approaching along the road from the Ossuary passes a couple of battered infantry shelters and a trench or two but nothing in the silent landscape really prepares him for the sight of the fort itself. A quarter of a mile across, its top a mass of shell holes, its deep ditch battered and uneven, picket posts and iron bars still protruding here and there, Fort Douaumont is a huge, defiant mass. It is not just a monument to military engineering. It is a monument to human courage and endurance under conditions of unimaginable privation, squalor and fear.

In 1925 the Douaumont volume of the German narrative history of the war, *Schlachten des Weltkrieges*, was published in Berlin. The final line of the flowing text says quite simply *Dieser Berg ist uns Schicksal geworden*: This hill became our fate. The line applies as much to the French as to the Germans. In fact, since Fort Douaumont was the inspiration for the Maginot Line, one can say that, in a sense, it became the fate of very many more people on both sides in a later war whose coming was as unimaginable in 1918 as the horror of Verdun is for us today.

ADVICE TO TOURERS

Getting to Verdun: Verdun lies roughly 450 kilometres southeast of Calais and can easily be reached by car via the A26 and the A4. There are also two possible train services into the city: the three hour journey via Chalons-en-Champagne, which requires a change of train, or the fifty nine minute high speed (TGV) service. Both services leave from the Gare de l'Est, Paris. The high speed train stops at the new Meuse TGV station, which is twenty two kilometres south of Verdun and is connected to the city centre by shuttle bus.

Getting to the battlefield: The battlefield sites are at a considerable distance from the city. At the time of writing there are plans for a summer tourist bus to run between the city and the battlefield. However, the bus that ran during the recent season did not include Fort Vaux in its itinerary, so

The Porte and the Pont Chaussée in 1916.

visitors wishing to visit that fort and the outlying sites mentioned in this book would still need a car or a bicycle. As car hire possibilities in Verdun are limited, train travellers might do better to consider hiring a car in one of the larger centres such as Rheims or Metz.

The Porte Chaussée.

Information about bike hire and walking routes is available from either the *Maison de Tourisme*, Place de la Nation, tel. 0033 3 29 86 14 18, verduntourisme@wanadoo.fr, or the new *Office de Tourisme*, 0033 3 29 84 55 55, tourisme@cc-verdun.fr, which is situated just over the road on the Ave. Général Mangin.

Please note that the firing range to the north of Fort Douaumont is in use on Mondays and Tuesdays between 8am and midnight. As this restricts access to the Douaumont sector, Tour No 1 cannot be walked on those days.

Ruins in Verdun.

Accommodation: The city offers accommodation ranging from three star hotels to camp sites. However, as car parking in the centre of Verdun is both restricted and fairly expensive, an out-of-town hotel may be a more attractive option. For a full list of accommodation, contact either of the tourist offices above or check this site: http://www.verdun-tourisme.com/www-sommaire_hotels-785-UK-FAMILLE.html.

Some bed and breakfast possibilities in the area are listed on: http://en.likhom.com/

Books and maps: The most useful general map of the wider area is the 1/200.000 Michelin Yellow Series No. 241 (Champagne-Ardennes). However, for getting around while at Verdun it is probably easier to use the 1/100.000 IGN (*Institut Géographique National*) Green Series Map No. 10 (Rheims-Verdun). The IGN No.10 stops immediately to the east of the battlefield but it is smaller and easier to handle than the Michelin No. 241, as well as being a larger scale. For a close study of the battlefield itself the best maps are either the special IGN battlefield map No. 3112 ET named *Forêts de Verdun et du Mort-Homme; Champ de Bataille de Verdun*, which is produced by the *Office National des Forêts*, or the IGN 1/25.000 Blue Series. Fort Douaumont is covered by IGN No. 3212 *Ouest* (Douaumont-Vaux). These are available in Verdun at the *Librairie Ducher* (the bookshop in the main shopping street) and may also be available on the battlefield. It is also possible to buy IGN maps direct from the website on: http://www.ign.fr

Trench maps: These are not so easy to get hold of but it is worth contacting the *Service Historique de la défense* at the Chateau de Vincennes, France, or the archives at the Memorial de Verdun, to find out what is available and whether photocopies may be obtained. The French official history of the war, named *Les Armées Françaises dans la Grande Guerre*, contains sector maps and these may be obtained at

Mémorial de Verdun.

a small charge from the archives at the Memorial. For the Fort Douaumont sector the most useful maps from the French official history are Map No. 16, Tome IV, 1st Vol., showing the successive fronts to the north of Verdun between 21-26 February 1916, Map No. 2, Tome IV, 2nd Vol., for the French attack of 22 May 1916 and Maps Nos. 4 and 5, Tome IV, 3rd Vol. showing the French and German units in line on the Right Bank on 24 October

The Ossuary.

1916. The disposition of French artillery for the October offensive is to be found on Map No. 6, Tome IV, 3rd Vol.

Clothing/footwear: Verdun can be very wet, so bring a rainproof jacket and a waterproof bag for camera, pencils and notebook. A torch is also useful. Forest paths are always muddy so make sure you have adequate stout, waterproof footwear. The forts are cool and damp, so carry a sweater or jacket even on a hot day. Make sure your tetanus jab is up to date and that you are properly covered for medical insurance. In summer, bring sun cream and plenty of mosquito repellent, including mosquito spray for your room.

Refreshments: There are a number of authorized picnic sites and the *Abri des Pélerins* café/restaurant, which is near the Ossuary, offers sandwiches, meals and drinks throughout the day. The *Abri* is open from February to mid-November but is likely to be closed on Mondays out of season. When closed, the nearest refreshment possibilities are in Verdun or Bras-sur-Meuse, so plan to carry a snack and plenty of water.

Toilet facilities: Toilet facilities on the battlefield are extremely limited. There are toilets behind the Ossuary, in the Memorial museum and at the *Abri des Pélerins* but they are only accessible during opening hours. There are no toilet facilities in the forts.

When to travel: Summer is likely to bring the best weather but the thick forest and dense undergrowth makes it difficult to get a feel for the terrain and the mosquitoes are a nuisance. Autumn and early spring are better, particularly the latter, when the organized hunting season is over. Surprising though it may seem, hunts can temporarily block access to large areas, including the main historical sites.

Winter weather: Particular care should be exercised in snow and icy weather, as the roads across the battlefield are unlikely to be cleared of snow, salted or gritted. This also applies to the minor roads taken by Tour No 4.

Road numbers: Some road numbers in the area have changed over the last few years. The N3 is now the D603 and the N18 is the D618. At the time of writing these changes are not reflected on the IGN maps

To obtain a view of Fort Douaumont: The thick forest covering the battlefield today makes it difficult to obtain a clear idea of the dominating position of Fort Douaumont or the strategic importance of the ridge on which it stands. This can be remedied to some extent by a visit to the top of the Ossuary tower. Although Fort Douaumont can only be glimpsed from the tower, the commanding position of the Douaumont-Froideterre ridge and its prime importance as an observatory become immediately clear. The sight of Fort Douaumont in the distance from the top of Fort Vaux will also give some idea of the strength of the position. Neither of them, however, can give any real feel for the overwhelming menace of the mighty structure that was felt by the Germans as they approached from the north in 1916. The best place to obtain that is from the top of Hill 378, which is a short walk from the D115 road from the destroyed village of Louvemont to Ornes (see Tour No 4). From here in clear weather the northwestern machine gun turret and 75mm turret of Fort Douaumont can be made out, as can the outline of the western ditch and – in winter and spring - the machine gun turret dominating the ridge to the east, which stands in a clump of high trees. This view leaves no doubt as to the commanding position of Fort Douaumont or the threat that it would have posed in 1916 if fully armed and garrisoned.

Where to start: For first time visitors a good place to start a tour of the sector is the *Memorial de Verdun*. This memorial museum, situated on the battlefield close to the destroyed village of Fleury, houses, among other things, an area of reconstructed, debris-strewn battlefield

Battlefield debris.

Fort Douaumont seen from the Memorial.

from which a visitor will gain some idea of the appearance of the terrain around the fort in 1916. Also on display are a maquette of Fort Douaumont and a relief map which shows the position of all the major and intermediary forts on the Left and Right Banks of the River Meuse. The museum shop in the entrance hall sells useful maps and books and outside there is a representative collection of guns, mortars and shells. In addition, from the steps of the Memorial, looking past the Ossuary along the ridge to the north, a visitor will be able to catch a first glimpse of the fort in the distance as a low, grey and apparently unbroken outline whose very smoothness gives no hint of the utter devastation that it suffered in 1916.

A note on time: During the Battle of Verdun, German time was normally one hour ahead of French time but during the summer of 1916 it was two hours ahead. Any specific time mentioned in this book is French time.

Warning: Most of the battlefield of Verdun is national forest and, while walking and cycling are encouraged, visitors should stick to the paths and trails and stay away from the edges of holes. **Collecting 'souvenirs', digging or using metal detectors are absolutely prohibited and subject to heavy fines.** Forts, shelters, dugouts and other positions are dangerous and should not be entered. Live ammunition, shells, grenades and mortar bombs should not be touched under any circumstances.

Separate sections at the end of this book contain information on guidebooks, other places of interest on the battlefield and useful addresses. Walks and car tours are described separately.

17

List of Maps and Plans

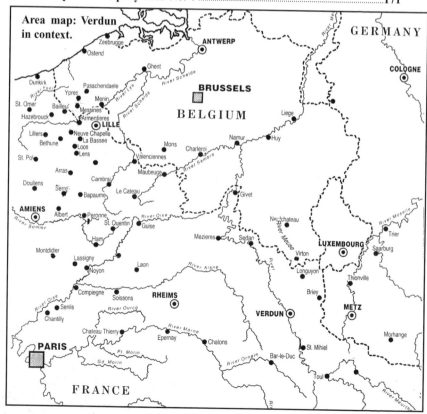

Area map: Verdun in context.

Chapter One

THE KEYSTONE OF THE ARCH

Standing at the crossroads of the traditional communication routes formed by the valley of the River Meuse and the ancient road from Metz to Rheims, Verdun has been from time immemorial the guardian of one of the historic gateways into France and a bulwark against invasion from the east. While man-made fortifications have added to the strength of the city, it is the geographical position of Verdun that is the key to its history, for it stands in the centre of a natural fortress of great strength.

The city is surrounded on all sides by flat topped limestone hills rising to 390 metres above sea level. On either side of the River Meuse the hills form long escarpments. While on their western sides the escarpments slope gently downwards, the eastern sides drop precipitously for several hundred feet. Over the ages, the action of streams running off the hills has sliced the hillsides into deep ravines, offering innumerable natural concealed positions for observation and defence. The winding course of the river has cut deeply into the escarpments on both sides of the valley, leaving interlocking spurs which project out onto the valley floor, dominating passage along the valley from either north or south and protecting the river crossings. The dense covering of forest on the heights and the thick undergrowth in the marshy bottom of the ravines form a natural barrier to easy movement in any direction and force communication lines to converge on the relatively small number of natural gateways which the streams have carved. Verdun thus lies in the centre of a terrain that is particularly formidable to an enemy from whichever direction he chooses to approach.

It is a very old city. The Romans fortified Verdun under the name of Verodunum Castrum but the roots of the town are much older than that. Its long history includes burning by Attila the Hun and capture by Clovis, as well as at least ten sieges. Annexed to Lorraine under the celebrated Treaty of Verdun of

Châtel gate, Verdun.

19

843AD which divided Charlemagne's empire into three parts, Verdun was for most of the medieval period a part of the German Empire. Becoming officially French in 1648, the medieval fortifications were modernized by the famous French military engineer, Vauban, whose citadel and city walls can still be seen today.

Vauban's urban defences were not modernized during the first half of the nineteenth century since at that time Verdun was not in the front line of defence against invasion from Germany. However, the position was dramatically changed in 1870 as a result of the defeat of France by the Prussians at Sedan during the Franco-Prussian War. Under the terms of the subsequent peace treaty, Germany annexed Alsace and a substantial part of Lorraine, thereby acquiring many of the fortresses of eastern France, including the nearby cities of Metz and Thionville. Verdun, which was situated forty kilometres from the new border and only separated from it by a marshy plain, suddenly found itself a vital frontier stronghold and the first line of defence against another German invasion.

Faced with the development of powerful German fortifications around Metz and Thionville (the *Moselstellung*) and the accompanying build-up of military force in the annexed parts of Lorraine, it became imperative for France to strengthen its eastern frontier. A defence committee was accordingly set up to study the question. The ideas adopted were those of General Raymond Séré de Rivières, an army engineer born in 1815 who, as commander of the Engineers at Metz in 1864, had begun the construction of the first modern detached forts around that city.

Fortification of the eastern frontier
Rather than fortifying the entire eastern frontier with permanent military works on a grand scale, the plan put forward by Séré de Rivières proposed to place opposite Germany two chains of fortresses, leaving between them an open gateway through which - it was believed - an invasion would have to be directed. The southern chain ran from Belfort on the Swiss border to Epinal while the northern chain extended from Verdun down the Meuse valley to Toul on the River Moselle. Between Toul and Epinal lay the unfortified gateway around the town of Charmes. The vital road and rail centres of Verdun, Toul, Epinal and Belfort, which buttressed the northern and southern ends of each system, were turned into fortified camps by the construction of rings of forts on strategic heights around each city.

The chain of forts between Verdun and Toul was intended to

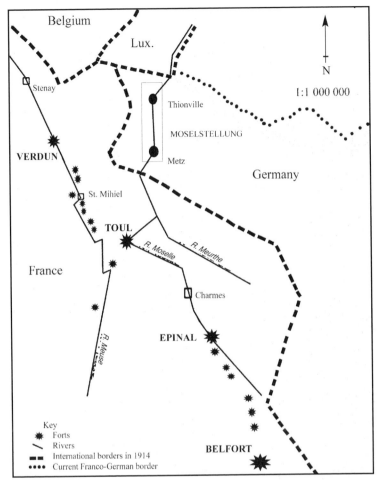

Forts and international boundaries in Eastern France after 1871.
Isabella Holstein

counterbalance the fortified camp formed by the German cities of Metz and Thionville, whose defences had been dramatically improved by an extensive fortress-building programme. The specific role of Verdun was threefold: to prevent the whole chain from being outflanked to the north, to form a bridgehead on the Meuse and to support possible French offensive action in the direction of Germany.

As Verdun's seventeenth century fortifications were inadequate to meet the demands of its new strategic role, a plan was drawn up for modern forts to be constructed on both sides of the river using commanding positions at least 150 metres above the plain and sufficiently far from the city to protect the city from enemy bombardment. The original project provided for a minimum of six

Ouvrage d'Eix. Built in 1888, this ouvrage is almost undamaged.

major forts supported by a further seven minor works (known as ouvrages) or by batteries. On the Right Bank, the new forts would dominate passage along the Meuse valley and control road and rail communications towards the German border and Metz. On the Left Bank, they would ensure security of operations towards the Argonne Forest and control the road to Paris, which was the only line of communication and retreat available to the French.

Before the plan could be implemented, however, the Franco-German crisis of 1875 brought a renewed threat of war and an immediate need to protect the city from bombardment by enemy troops over open sights. The original long-term project was abandoned and seven redoubts - later known as the 'panic forts' of Belleville, Saint-

Entrance to Fort Belleville.

Michel, Belrupt, Dugny, Regret, La Chaume and Marre - were hurriedly constructed on the heights overlooking Verdun where visible Prussian batteries had been established during the sieges of 1792 and 1870. The end of the crisis brought a return to the aims of the original plan and between 1876 and 1879 four forts were constructed to cover the approaches to Verdun from the north and east: Tavannes, Souville, Le Rozelier and Haudainville. A further eight forts and small ouvrages were built between 1881 and 1885.

Fort Douaumont

In preparing his project, Séré de Rivières had noted the remarkable defensive position formed by the high ridge close to the village of Douaumont. His original plan had provided for the construction of a fort at the point known as the *Signal de Douaumont*, 395.5 metres above sea level, where it dominated the approach to the city from the northeast. However, it was only in 1885 that work began on the site previously known to the Gallo-Romans as *Divus-Mons*, the sacred hill.

As originally constructed Fort Douaumont was polygonal in shape, measuring 400 metres from east to west and 300 metres from north to south. It was built of dressed limestone blocks that were one and a half metres thick and covered by three to five metres of earth. Surrounding the fort on all sides was a wide dry ditch roughly six metres deep which was crossed by a drawbridge. Like other forts of the period, caponiers flanked the ditch and a ravelin and guard house commanded the entrance. The artillery was mounted on the parapet in the open air. Two barrack blocks provided accommodation on two floors for almost

Entrance to Fort Génicourt, another Séré de Rivières fort to the south of Verdun. Note that the drawbridge is still intact.

Ditch of Fort Belleville with caponier on the left and counterscarp wall on the right.

900 officers and men and included medical facilities, kitchens, store rooms, magazines and the commandant's quarters.

The artillery revolution

Even before construction was completed, the traditional stone-built fort was rendered obsolete by developments in explosives and artillery. Firstly, the development of the air-burst shrapnel shell in 1880 made life extremely dangerous for unprotected guns and their crews. Secondly, the time fuze, which appeared in 1883, allowed a shell to penetrate into the body of a fort before exploding. More important, however, was the invention in 1885 of melinite, a high explosive of much greater power than the black powder previously used for charging shells. Parallel with these developments, improvements were also taking place in the design of guns and shells that led to increased range and velocity as well as higher calibres, improved rates of fire and greater accuracy. The increased destructive power of the shells when fired from the new guns and howitzers was devastating to earth-covered masonry forts. New ideas were thus urgently needed for the protection and defence of the forts.

To protect the artillery, the parapet guns were removed and placed in the intervals between the forts where they were covered by flanking fire from either side. With that, the forts ceased to be long-range batteries and became infantry support points and observation posts. Over the next few years an extensive network of infantry works and batteries was constructed throughout the whole sector to protect the intervals and support the forts. Reserve infantry positions and underground magazines were also created and water supplies, roads and narrow gauge railways improved.

To protect the forts themselves, however, some means had to be found of strengthening the original construction. Experiments carried out during 1886-1887 showed that a layer of earth at least ten metres deep would be needed to protect traditional forts from the new high explosive shells. However, further tests demonstrated that concrete was an effective protection for masonry provided that it was laid on a bed of sand and covered with a thick layer of earth. The composition of this 'special concrete' was 400 kilograms of cement for 0.300 cubic metres of sand and 0.900 cubic metres of aggregate which was hand crushed to a size of between forty and seventy millimetres.

Fort Douaumont is modernized

The task of modernizing the Verdun forts began in 1887 with Fort Douaumont, whose prime position protected the approaches to the city from the north and east and, in particular, from Metz. It was a gigantic task. The earth covering was first removed and the masonry was strengthened with pillars and concrete supports before being covered by a buffer of sand approximately one metre thick. Then, using for the first time a 'continuous pour' process, a thick layer of special concrete was poured on top of the sand. The eastern side of the barracks, some of the artillery bunkers and the tunnel into the barracks from the main entrance were covered with one and a half metres of concrete. The western side of the barracks and the remaining artillery bunkers, which were intended to form a strong 'keep' or redoubt for last ditch defence, received a covering two and a half metres thick. After completion, the

The merlon in 2001. The shell damage to the front shows the layers of masonry, sand and concrete.

CONCRETE REINFORCEMENT   SAND BUFFER   CONCRETE REINFORCEMENT   ORIGINAL MASONRY ARCH   SAND BUFFER

The western ditch. The steep bank on the left is the inner wall of the ditch.

whole of the concrete carapace was covered with a layer of earth between one and four metres deep. In 1888 a thick layer of special concrete was also applied to the open southern façade of the barracks. All in all, between April 1887 and November 1888 the work of strengthening Fort Douaumont required approximately 28,000 cubic metres of concrete and a team of some sixty construction workers.

To protect Fort Douaumont further, earth was banked up around the lower floor of the barrack block, covering it completely and effectively burying half the fort. The upper floor was now at ground level. To make the ditch less vulnerable to bombardment, the scarp wall was replaced by a sloping earth bank. To defend the ditch, strong, concrete galleries were constructed in the counterscarp, facing the fort itself. Armed with revolver guns and light cannon and later with searchlights, these galleries – single at the northern corners but double at the apex

Entrance blockhouse after shelling in February 1915. Note the gun embrasures on either side of the entrance.

of the fort - were designed to sweep with enfilading fire any enemy who managed to penetrate into the ditch. Connected to the barracks by long underground tunnels, the counterscarp galleries could be reinforced regardless of enemy fire. The original gateway was scrapped and a new entrance - an independent blockhouse protected by double flanking galleries and a drawbridge - was constructed in the gorge (south) side of the fort. From the blockhouse a tunnel ran under the rampart to an entrance on the lower floor of the fort.

The armament of the fort

The original plan for the armament of Fort Douaumont had provided for twenty guns mounted on the parapet but the revolution in high explosives and artillery in the 1880s meant that henceforward guns had to be protected if they were to remain operational at all times. As a first step, ten of the guns were dispersed in batteries outside the fort but the introduction of steel-reinforced concrete in 1897 made it possible to construct shell proof gun positions in the fort itself.

The first protected guns at Fort Douaumont were installed in 1902-1903 in a new type of strong concrete bunker known, from the experimental range on which it was first tested, as a Bourges Casemate (*Casemate de Bourges*). Embedded in the southwest corner of the superstructure and shielded from direct fire by a long wall forming a protective wing, this bunker was strengthened with a layer of concrete almost two metres thick. It was armed with two quick-firing 75mm field guns installed in two chambers placed in echelon, whose embrasures allowed for fire in one direction only. The fixed guns, which had a range of 5,500 metres, were sited so as to cover the southwestern approach to the fort and to cover with flanking fire the defensive works situated along the ridge between Fort Douaumont and the *Ouvrage de Froideterre*. An observation post and magazines completed the installation.

The construction of the Bourges Casemate marked the beginning of the period that turned Fort Douaumont into a modern, armoured fort of enormous strength. Between 1902 and 1913, further armament was

Bourges Casemate at Fort Vaux. Note guns visible in the embrasures.

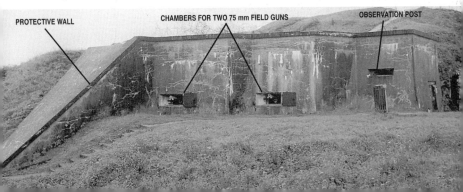

PROTECTIVE WALL   CHAMBERS FOR TWO 75 mm FIELD GUNS   OBSERVATION POST

Destroyed observation turret at the Ouvrage de Thiaumont showing the thickness of the steel dome.

provided in the form of guns housed in retractable steel turrets of very advanced design which, by rotating through 360°, covered all the approaches to the fort. The turrets were activated by a vertical movement that raised them into the firing position and lowered them again once the gun had ceased firing. Raising the turret exposed the gun embrasures and allowed the guns inside to fire. When retracted, the guns were hidden from view and entirely protected by a steel dome which, in the case of the bigger turrets, was strong enough to withstand even direct hits by the heaviest shells. The turret was set in a reinforced concrete unit that also housed the activating machinery, magazine, replacement guns and range-finding equipment. Each one was coupled with an observation post protected by a dome of steel twenty-five centimetres thick and connected to the gun by speaking tube or telephone.

Four such turrets were installed in Fort Douaumont and linked to the barracks by underground tunnels. Two lighter models housed twin eight millimetre Hotchkiss machine guns that were mounted one above the other and fired alternately to avoid overheating. Intended for the

Machine gun turret with observation post in foreground.

Cupola of 155mm gun turret. The cupola is raised half way to the firing position. Note the gun embrasure just visible on the right.

close defence of the fort, the machine guns were installed at the northeast and northwest corners of the superstructure where the visibility was best. On the eastern side of the fort a short-barrelled 155mm gun capable of firing three rounds a minute over a range of 7,500 metres protected the vital north and northeast fronts. An armoured observation post at the entrance to the turret communicated with it through a speaking tube while another some distance away communicated with the gun crew by telephone. Twin short-barrelled 75mm guns housed in a similar turret in the escarpment to the north completed the armament. The 75mm guns, which together were capable of firing more than twenty two rounds a minute over a range of 5,500 metres, were intended to sweep the intervals between the forts. Their considerable firepower more than compensated for the dispersion of the remainder of the fort's artillery in external batteries. By 1913, all the gun turrets, observation posts and the Bourges Casemate had been linked to the barrack block by strong underground passages so that they could be accessed at all times without going outside.

Mighty though it was, Fort Douaumont formed only one element in a strong and extensive 'centre of resistance' which also included

Almost all that is left of the Ouvrage d'Hardaumont, one of the six ouvrages of the Douaumont defensive sector.

Douaumont village, six *ouvrages*, five combat shelters, six concrete batteries, an underground shelter for reserves, two ammunition depots and a whole series of concrete infantry entrenchments. A revolving turret for twin 155s on the slopes to the south of the fort and another for a 75mm gun on the ridge to the east should have completed the defence but neither emplacement was complete when war broke out. A machine gun was mounted in the observation post on the ridge, while the incomplete 75mm gun turret became a shelter.

Access to the fort

Fort Douaumont was an immense structure, measuring almost 300 metres from north to south and 400 metres from east to west. It was protected on all sides by an open glacis offering wide fields of fire in every direction and surrounded by a belt of wire thirty metres deep, which was attached to metal picket posts set in concrete. At the top of the glacis, a line of stout spiked railings two and a half metres high ran along the counterscarp. On the floor of the ditch – approximately six metres below the top of the counterscarp - a further line of railings was set at an angle along the base of the scarp. The outer wall of the ditch was strengthened by a facing of masonry on three sides of the fort, but on the south side, where the inner wall was strengthened and provided with flanking blockhouses, it consisted of only a bank of earth.

The fort was accessed by means of a wagon road that led up the glacis on the south side of the fort, passed a guard house and came down in the ditch close to the main entrance or 'peacetime gate'. The road then ran across a drawbridge and entered a tunnel under the rampart. This led to the 'wartime gate', which allowed direct entry to the lower floor of the barracks. At the end of the tunnel, two ramps provided access to the upper floor of the barracks and to the covered wagon roads that passed through the barrack block at each end. Emerging from the barracks on the north side, the wagon roads became the *Rue du Rempart*, which served the adjoining artillery shelters and ammunition depots. Access to the fort on foot was also possible by

Section through Fort Douaumont from south to north.

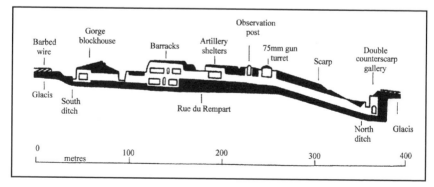

Guard house at Fort Douaumont.

means of steps cut into the rampart, which led to a footbridge spanning the gap between the tunnel and the wartime gate. On the top of the rampart, two light steel domes allowed for observation over the south side of the fort

The barrack block was a two storey building. The lower floor, known as the 'wartime barracks', comprised the fort's administrative services, siege headquarters for the commandant and his staff, depots, magazines and two groups of cisterns each holding 520 cubic metres of water. The upper floor, or 'peacetime barracks', provided accommodation for the garrison of 850, workshops, magazines and kitchens as well as a bakery and an infirmary. Staircases or metal ladders linked the two floors and on each level the barrack rooms opened onto a principal corridor. On the upper floor the corridor ran throughout the whole length of the barracks and joined the covered wagon roads at either end of the building.

One year before the outbreak of the war, Fort Douaumont was complete. The strongest and most modern of all the forts around Verdun, it was the cornerstone of the whole defensive system. Its construction, modernization and armament had required a total of twenty eight years and had cost 6,100,000 gold francs.

The Verdun sector

As regards the Verdun sector as a whole, thirty years of continuous development and extension of the defensive system around the city meant that when war broke out Verdun was defended by a double ring of twenty eight principal forts and ouvrages. They were situated at distances varying from two and a half to eight kilometres from the Citadel and most of them had been modernized and strengthened by a partial covering of concrete. The forts and ouvrages were mutually supporting, so that any enemy attacking one of them would also come

31

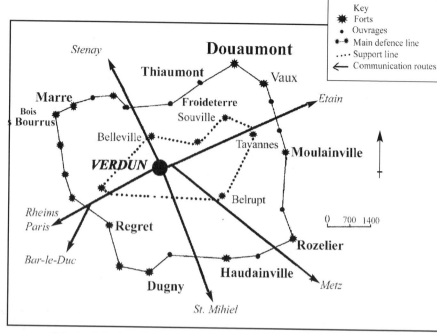

Principal forts and ouvrages around Verdun in 1916.

under fire from those on the flanks. The forts of the outer ring, whose circumference was forty five kilometres, disposed of seventy nine guns in shell proof turrets or casemates and their ditches were protected by more than 200 revolver guns and light cannon. Six of the forts were armed with 155mm guns under modern retractable turrets while a further fourteen comprised retractable turrets for twin 75s.

Further protection was provided by a vast network of concrete infantry shelters, armoured observation posts, batteries, concrete entrenchments, command posts and underground shelters for reserves which were constructed in the intervals between the forts. Magazines and depots were dispersed throughout the area and at certain strategic sites searchlights illuminated the ravines. Three pumping stations ensured a permanent water supply. Almost 1000 guns, mortars and machine guns were in position with a further 250 in reserve and their interlinking fields of fire protected every approach to the city. Most of the forts and ouvrages were linked by telegraph and telephone and the whole fortified camp was served by a narrow gauge railway system and a network of strategic routes of enormous extent which offered secure communications, provisioning and supply. On mobilization, the garrison comprised 66,000 men and rations for six months.

By 1914 the construction and armament of the whole system, excluding the citadel and the city itself, had cost some 127 million gold francs. Verdun was by far the strongest and most modern fortress city in France and – on paper at least – a position of overwhelming strength. It soon had an opportunity to prove itself.

In the weeks following the outbreak of war in August 1914, the Germans tried to circumvent the fortified camp of Verdun rather than face its guns. However, their attempts to outflank the sector to the west and southeast were unsuccessful and the end of the First Battle of the Marne left Verdun in the centre of a wide salient. It was a dangerous position to be in. While failing to outflank the sector, the German offensives of September 1914 had destroyed or reduced the main supply and communication lines into Verdun, leaving the fortified city dependent for reliable supply upon a single metre-gauge railway line and one road. With the northern apex of the salient only twenty four kilometres from the main German supply line on the Western Front, it was clear that further offensives against Verdun could be expected.

The Gündell-Turm.
H.P. von Müller's Estate

As early as September 1914, Fort Douaumont's 155mm gun was in action against German positions to the north of the sector. The Germans soon replied with a barrage of medium and heavy calibre shells that caused some slight damage but left the fort's vital organs unscathed. The operation was observed by a prominent guest, Crown Prince Wilhelm of Germany, who had been invited by the commander of V Reserve Corps, General Erich von Gündell, to view the shooting from his newly built observation tower, the 'Gündell-Turm'. The French were not impressed and the tower soon became a favourite target of French gunners.

In December 1914 the 155mm gun was again in action, this time against the *Jumelles d'Ornes*, two hills that formed an important German observation post to the northeast of the sector. That brought retaliation from the Germans in February

33

BOURGES CASEMATE   MERLON
FOOTBRIDGE

SOUTH SIDE OF BARRACKS

A German photograph of Fort Douaumont at the start of the battle. Note the damage caused by German heavy shells in February 1915. Mémorial de Verdun

1915 in the form of a 'shooting match' (*Wettschiessen*) between two of their biggest guns - a 420mm Krupp mortar and a 380mm 'Long Max' naval gun - during which thirty four huge projectiles were hurled against the fort and its immediate surroundings. Despite a great column of smoke which rose above the glacis and at first led the Germans to believe that the fort had been put out of action, only limited damage was done. On the eastern side of the barracks where the concrete carapace was only one and a half metres thick, three shells falling close together brought down the roof of the bakery and a nearby corridor, while the blast from a fourth fissured the floor and walls of the gallery leading to the 75mm turret. The guns, however, were unharmed. One 420mm shell striking the reinforced concrete collar of the 155mm turret left a deep hole but only slightly affected the turret mechanism and repairs were carried out within a day or two. Another fell without exploding close to the *Rue du Rempart*, where it was defused and sent to Paris for exhibition.

The fact that such a shell had hit the concrete covering of the fort and failed to explode probably encouraged the French High Command in its comfortable belief that the most powerful of the forts around Verdun was impregnable. Indeed, had the whole mighty system not been disarmed in the second year of the war, that belief might well have proved correct.

Chapter Two

DOUAUMONT HAS FALLEN!

The reason why the forts were disarmed was quite simple. When the German heavy artillery smashed the Belgian forts in August 1914 it also shattered the French High Command's faith in fixed fortifications. Seeing the damage wrought at Liège by Krupp's new super-heavy howitzers, the High Command concluded that because even modern works could be destroyed by the devastating power of the enemy's artillery, forts no longer had any value. In fact, it was argued, they would only serve to attract the heaviest shelling, in which case the guns, supplies and garrisons tied up there could be better used elsewhere.

Accordingly, by a decree signed in August 1915, the fortified camp of Verdun was reclassified and given an essentially defensive role. The military governor was instructed that the sector should not be defended for itself and that he should not allow himself to be besieged there. Within a short time, steps were taken to strip the forts of their garrisons, guns, ammunition and supplies. By October 1915 forty three heavy batteries and eleven field gun batteries, plus 128,000 rounds, had been sent to other fronts and virtually the only guns remaining were those mounted under the revolving turrets.

Despite its supreme importance for the defence of the sector, Fort Douaumont was not spared. As early as October 1914 the ammunition reserves had been partially requisitioned; now the guns were removed from the Bourges Casemate, the machine gun turrets and the nearby field batteries. The garrison was sent into line in the Woëvre and the Bourges Casemate lost its gunners.

At the same time, army engineers at Verdun were ordered to prepare for the possible destruction of the vital organs of Fort Douaumont in order to prevent them from falling into enemy hands. The plan that was drawn up concerned the revolving turrets, Bourges Casemate and observation posts, as well as a section of the gorge wall. Over five thousand kilograms of explosives were brought up to the fort and work began on preparing mine chambers under the gorge. A pioneer sergeant sent up to organise the mining arrived in the fort on 25th February, the very day on which it fell to the Germans. An officer who was to have joined him later in the day disappeared en route.

The south side of the fort at the beginning of 1916, looking towards the 155mm gun turret. The 1915 shell damage has not been repaired. H.P. von Müller's Estate

When the Battle of Verdun began on 21 February 1916, all that was left of the once mighty armament of Fort Douaumont were the 75mm and 155mm turret guns, the light cannon defending the ditch and a dense field of wire on the glacis. The fort itself was regarded as nothing more than a barracks. The bombardments of 1915 had damaged the main gate, blocked the drawbridge and left doors broken or swinging on their hinges. The 'garrison' had been reduced to a handful of men under the command of a sixty year old white bearded *Gardien de Batterie* (warrant officer) named Chenot.

Elderly he might have been but Chenot took his responsibilities seriously. With the withdrawal of the garrison in 1915 Chenot found himself alone in the fort. Believing that the remaining turret guns could still be useful, Chenot asked for gunners to be sent up to serve them and when territorials arrived who were unfamiliar with the type of guns in the fort, he set about teaching them their trade. Chenot was also careful whom he let in. When, in early February 1916, an unknown officer presented himself at the gate of Fort Douaumont, he was refused entry. In vain the officer protested that he was General Chrétien, commander of XXX Corps, and that the fort fell within his sector. Chenot was unmoved: 'I'm sorry, General...I have not been informed of your visit. I ought to have you arrested as a spy...'

As General Becker, Deputy Chief of Staff to General Chrétien, wryly remarked, 'Oh yes, Fort Douaumont was well guarded'.

Compared to other areas of the Western Front, the Verdun sector

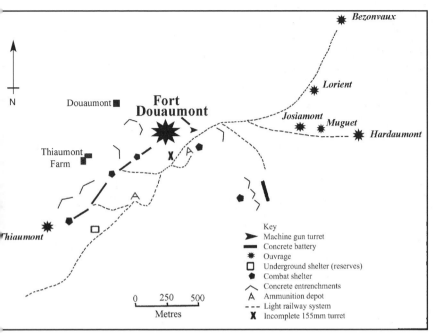

The Douaumont fortified sector.

had remained fairly quiet during 1915 and the urgent need for men and materials in more hard pressed sectors had drained the salient of its resources. This drain was reflected in the state of the defences. General Chrétien, who undertook a tour of inspection in the sector on taking up his duties in January 1916, discovered to his horror a *'terrain à catastrophes'*. With the exception of one or two sectors, the trench systems were decaying for lack of maintenance, roads and tracks had become swamps, material and equipment rotted and rusted in the open air. Instead of a continuous trench line there was a series of 'centres of resistance' separated from one another by open intervals crossed by thin wire entanglements or other obstacles and covered by machine gun and rifle fire. The rare communication trenches were shallow and there were few solidly organised command posts or entrenched field works, well supplied and able to resist encirclement.

The city seemed unaffected by the year of bitter trench warfare that had afflicted other parts of the front. Arriving in Verdun on 30 January 1916 a young artillery officer, *Aspirant* Texier, found that it had an air of a garrison town on a Sunday afternoon. Just three weeks before the start of the longest battle of the war, Texier had to make a serious effort to remember that he really was at the front.

Gun pit in Warphémont Wood, from which a German 380mm naval gun fired the first shot in the Battle of Verdun.

The battle begins

At 7.12am on 21 February 1916 the 380mm 'Long Max' naval gun in Warphémont Wood raised its long barrel and fired the first shell in the Battle of Verdun. It signalled the start of a ferocious bombardment and by the end of the first day the German infantry had largely penetrated the French forward positions. For the next three days the battered French troops were driven back towards the fortress line until by the evening of 24 February the total collapse of the defence on the Right Bank seemed imminent. Disregarding advice from local commanders that only an immediate withdrawal to the Left Bank would save the situation, the French Commander-in-Chief, General Joffre, ordered that there should be no retreat. The entire Second Army, then in reserve, was immediately transferred to Verdun to defend the Right Bank. Its commander, General Philippe Pétain, arrived during the evening on 25 February and set up his headquarters at Souilly, a small town situated to the south of the city astride the vital road from Bar-le-Duc to Verdun.

By the time he did so, however, Fort Douaumont, the key to the entire defensive system around Verdun, had already fallen into German hands. To make matters worse, it had fallen without a fight.

General Philippe Pétain.
The Liberty Memorial Museum, Kansas City, Missouri

25 February: Fort Douaumont

To German troops arriving in the sector, Fort Douaumont was an impressive sight. From whatever direction they came the view was dominated by the long angular shape of the fort. They murmured that it surely contained a strong garrison and powerful guns and that its capture would demand a great sacrifice. They called it *der Berg*, the hill, or sometimes - from its shape - *der Sargdeckel*, an altogether more threatening name meaning a coffin lid.

Impressive Fort Douaumont might have been from the outside but its appearance was deceptive. When the special garrisons were withdrawn in August 1915, responsibility for the defence of the forts – including Fort Douaumont - fell to local commanders and troops in the field. However, the speed of the German onslaught during the first few days of the battle and the rapid disintegration of the French front forced the French High Command to see that the forts might still have a role to play in supporting troops in the field. Accordingly, on 24 February, General Chrétien issued an urgent order for them to be re-garrisoned and defended at all costs. At the time it was given, however, responsibility for the sector was about to pass from Chrétien's XXX Corps to XX Corps, and in the chaos of the battle the order was not transmitted to the divisional commanders.

On the evening of 24 February, Fort Douaumont was attracting particularly heavy shellfire and the commander of 306 Brigade, in whose sector the fort lay, ordered the troops to give it a wide berth. The sole occupants of the fort were a miscellaneous group under Chenot's command whose main concern was simply to survive. In addition to the fifty six Territorial gunners, there was an infantryman left behind to trim and light the fort's kerosene lamps, a working party engaged since 10 February in constructing an observation post and six gunners from an external battery of short-barrelled 155s. They were joined on 25 February by the pioneer sergeant. There was no officer, and Chenot was in command.

Although the little garrison was safe inside Fort Douaumont, conditions were far from pleasant there during the bombardment. A rain of medium and heavy calibre shells had battered the fort almost continuously from 21 February. It had withstood the hammering but while life under the concrete carapace was bearable, it was dreadfully demoralizing. Day after day the shells screamed down with a noise like an express train, blowing out the lamps and leaving the men in darkness. Clouds of suffocating dust and fumes filled barrack rooms and corridors and made breathing difficult. The reverberations were so great that for the garrison it was like being inside an enormous drum. However, they were safe underground and it was there that everyone who was not involved in operating the 155mm gun took refuge as often as they could.

Situation outside the fort: French units

On the morning of 25 February the situation in front of Fort Douaumont was as follows: the 44th Infantry Regiment held Bezonvaux village, approximately three kilometres to the northeast of the fort. The 4th Battalion of Chasseurs was in position southwest of Bezonvaux, while the 2nd Chasseurs were in the southwestern sector of La Vauche Wood. Two battalions of the 95th Infantry Regiment and units from the 2nd and 3rd Zouaves were holding Hill 347 and the approaches to Hill 378, while five hundred metres from the fort the third battalion held Douaumont village. One battalion of the 208th Infantry Regiment had moved forward from positions to the northeast of Fort Douaumont. They were believed to be in Hassoule Wood, close

Approximate French and German positions on the morning of 25 February 1916.

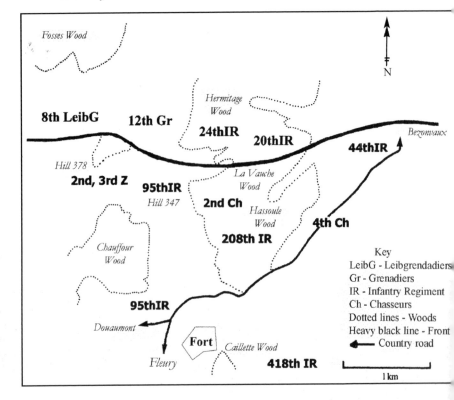

behind the Chasseurs, and had established advance posts at the northern edges of the woods to the east of Bezonvaux.

Southeast of the fort, the 418th Infantry was digging in between Caillette Wood and Fausse-Côte Ravine. One kilometre to the southwest, 110 Brigade with elements of the 51st Division was regrouping around Thiaumont farm, while 3 Moroccan Brigade was in support close to Fort Souville.

The ridge to the east of the fort was not occupied by French troops and neither was the fort itself.

German units

Opposite the French, in positions stretching eastwards from Fosses Wood to Hermitage Wood, were units of the 8th Leibgrenadiers, 12th Grenadiers and 24th, 64th and 20th Infantry Regiments. They all formed part of General von Lochow's III Corps, which was raised in Brandenburg and based in Berlin.

It had been a bitterly cold and snowy night and in Hermitage Wood the Brandenburgers stamped their feet and swung their arms to get warm before going in search of breakfast. Those who still had iron rations were fortunate; the others went in search of discarded packs since the field kitchen was once again nowhere to be seen.

The morning was bright and sunny. At the southern edge of Hermitage Wood a long ravine widened out and the ground rose gently to Hill 347 some four hundred metres away to the south. There was no cover and in the bright morning light the Brandenburgers could clearly see French troops digging in as calmly as if they were on exercises. To the watching Germans they seemed to be unaware of the presence of the enemy until their work was interrupted by machine gun and trench mortar fire. From Hill 347 a wide spur running in a northeasterly direction prevented the Germans from seeing the second French position which ran across a hilltop to the west of Hassoule Wood, five hundred metres further south. It also prevented them from seeing Fort

The view north of the fort, looking towards French and German positions.

HILL 378   HILL 347   HERMITAGE WOOD   STRAWBERRY RAVINE

Douaumont, which rose above Hill 347 at the end of a long open ridge.

The early morning passed quietly enough. French reconnaissance planes passed overhead and German patrols moving forward from Hermitage Wood reported that the French were working faster to deepen and extend their new positions. The 2nd Battalion of the 24th (5, 6, 7 and 8 Companies) pushed through Hermitage Wood and sought cover in the thick undergrowth by the track which ran along its southern edge. On their left, the 3rd Battalion (9, 10, 11 and 12 Companies) came up to relieve the 64th Infantry, which went into Corps reserve. The 1st and 3rd battalions of the 20th Infantry were holding the eastern end of La Vauche Wood, with the 2nd Battalion covering their left flank towards Bezonvaux. On the extreme right, the 1st Battalion of the 12th Grenadiers was moving forward but was still a kilometre behind.

Artillery preparation began at 9am and continued throughout the morning without any order to advance being received by the front line units. Hours passed and the waiting troops began to suffer from both the enemy artillery and their own guns. At 1pm the bombardment increased in intensity and finally the long-awaited order was received. At 3pm all units were to advance to a line running from the southeastern corner of Chauffour Wood to the trenches southwest of Hassoule Wood, where they were to halt on a line 800 metres from the fort. At the same time the artillery barrage was to lift to Fort Douaumont and be maintained there until darkness fell. The assault on the fort would be made the following day.

It was the 24th Infantry that had the fort directly in their sights and they were disappointed to find that they were not to be storming the fort that day. Their disappointment was greatly increased a few minutes later by a further order from Army Corps staff which changed the sectors of operations, so that instead of advancing directly on the fort, the 24th was to swing to the left around its northeastern shoulder. As a result, the honour of taking Fort Douaumont on 26 February would fall to the 12th Grenadiers.

The 24th Infantry Regiment – its full name was 'Infantry Regiment 'Grand Duke Friedrich Franz II of Mecklenburg-Schwerin' No. 24' - was insulted. A proud regiment with a centuries-old reputation for courage and a history of dashing exploits since August 1914, it was not the first time that the 24th had been at Verdun. On 13 September 1873 they had been the last of the occupying troops to march out of the city after the end of the Franco-Prussian War and as far as the 24th was concerned, that made Fort Douaumont theirs by right. That it should now fall to the Grenadiers was simply unjust.

Jump-off: 3pm on 25 February

The 24th was to advance in two waves. On the 2nd Battalion front, 8 and 6 Companies were to lead off, followed by 5 and 7 Companies. On the 3rd Battalion front, 9 and 10 Companies would advance ahead of 11 and 12 Companies.

A last-minute hitch in communications meant that orders did not reach the flanking regiments in time so that when zero hour came, the 24th advanced unsupported. As a result, 8 Company waited anxiously for several minutes for the 12th Grenadiers to appear before moving

The German assault on Fort Douaumont based on the account in *Schlachten des Weltkrieges.*

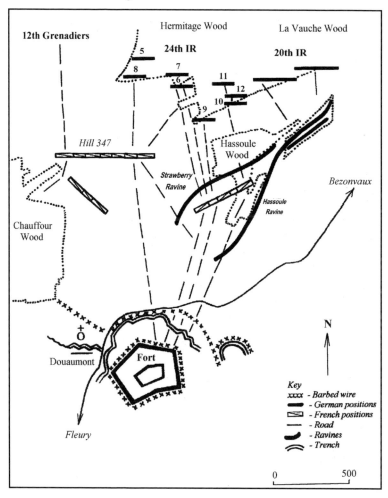

off with their right flank in the air, closely followed by 5 Company. It was almost fifteen minutes after zero hour before the impatient Grenadiers received their orders to advance and by then 8 Company was far ahead.

Supported by machine guns firing from the edge of Hermitage Wood, the 24th rushed the French positions in the woods and along Hill 347, capturing guns and scattering the French troops. Many were taken prisoner, while others fled away towards the eastern side of the fort. Finding themselves outflanked on the right, French units on Hill 347 fell back rapidly towards Douaumont village. The glacis of the fort was left empty of defenders.

In little more than twenty minutes advanced detachments of the 24th reached all their assigned objectives. Surprised by their success, and delighted to find the situation so different from the hard fighting of the last four days, the Brandenburgers set off across open ground in joyous pursuit of the fleeing French. Within seconds, they ran into crackling machine gun fire from the tower of Douaumont church. The Brandenburgers – by now all units were mixed up - scattered for cover into nearby woodland and a long defile named Strawberry Ravine which ran southwest in the direction of the fort. Using the cover provided by the ravine, they reached the country road from Douaumont village to Bezonvaux.

The Brandenburgers had gone well beyond their objectives for the day. They had lost touch with the units on either side of them, and now they faltered. Ahead of them, they could see Fort Douaumont clearly. The prisoners taken earlier had said that the fort was only lightly manned and it seemed absolutely silent, apart from the 155mm gun which was still firing harmlessly over their heads at some distant target.

Suddenly the German bombardment started again. The speed of the storm troopers' advance had taken everyone by surprise and although signallers with 6 and 7 Companies, pushing telephone lines up to the front in the wake of the assaulting infantry, had informed the artillery that the advance wave of troops was only a few hundred metres from the fort, the messages had not been believed. Hearing, however, that the assigned objectives had been taken and wishing to exploit their success, Army Corps command ordered *Massenfeuer auf Fort Douaumont* and the heavy howitzer batteries swung into increased action.

In the circumstances, it was as dangerous to stay where they were as to go on and - quite independently of one another - two officers of the

2nd Battalion decided to ignore their clear orders and to head towards the fort. They were an East Prussian reservist, Lieutenant Eugen Radtke, aged twenty four, of 6 Company and *Hauptmann* Hans Joachim Haupt, a thirty nine year old regular soldier commanding 7 Company.

The bombardment was increasing in intensity and the men took cover from the shells wherever they could. Radtke and Haupt fired flares, hoping that the artillery observers would see them. It was in vain. Snow was falling and in the fading light neither the green flares nor even Haupt's last desperate white ones could be seen. Beyond the road was a belt of wire protecting a trench that ran around the fort. The trench, which was unoccupied, seemed to offer a promise of better cover than the open ground where they now stood. One of Haupt's men handed his rifle to a friend and began to cut a way through the wire to reach it. Others followed, including Radtke and Haupt. They spread out along the trench, wondering what would happen next.

Lieutenant Eugen Radtke.
H.P. von Müller's Estate

Forward, the fort is ours!

Haupt realized the dangerous position they were in but he could see there was no way back. Climbing out of the trench and pointing in the direction of the fort he shouted to the men to follow him. Suddenly, Lieutenant Voigt, a reservist with the 22nd Pioneers, spotted an electrified wire. Lacking insulated wire cutters, he took a pickaxe to smash a glass insulator attached to a wooden picket post. No sparks came from the broken wire and, seeing that there was no current, the men began to climb out of the trench and on through the second entanglement, scratching and tearing their uniforms and hands.

As they did so, the machine gun fire from the direction of Douaumont died away. The defenders of Douaumont village had seen the green and white flares rising into the

Hauptmann Haupt.
Bundesarchiv Koblenz. Bild 183/R16739

air and wondered at the lack of response from the fort. Now as they peered into the gloom they saw just a couple of hundred metres away what appeared to be small groups of men well ahead of where the Germans had last been seen, hurrying in the direction of the fort. Incredulously the French watched them disappear into the barrage and for a few minutes they held their fire, believing them to be retreating Zouaves who had been sent up earlier that day to reinforce Hill 378. In accordance with the orders issued to storm troops the Germans had unscrewed the spikes from their helmets and in the dim light the unusual profile of the headgear had led the French to mistake the German soldiers for retreating French troops. By the time they changed their minds it was too late; the first group of Germans had safely reached the top of the glacis close to the northern apex of the fort.

Into the fort

But there they met a fresh obstacle - the two and a half metre high iron railing that ran along the top of the wall on the outer side of the ditch. The men spread out along the railing and a sharp-eyed NCO from 12 Company spotted a breach blasted by a German shell which had left a pile of rubble at the bottom of the wall. In the absence of ropes or ladders Radtke and Sergeant Wiedenhus, 6 Company, knotted their rifle slings together. Then, taking his courage in both hands, Radtke let himself down into the ditch, the first German officer into the fort. As he reached the ditch, *Gefreiter* Baack, also of 6 Company, who had climbed down through a breach at the northeast corner, ran round to join him.

It was 4pm. Radtke was fully aware of the danger that he was in. From his training at Fort Königsberg he knew only too well how modern forts were defended and he fully expected to be caught in a hail of fire from the nearby counterscarp gallery. All was quiet, however. Sergeant Wiedenhus slithered down after him and others followed. Then from the bottom of the ditch Radtke heard someone shout that Haupt was down. A shell exploding on the top of the wall had sent earth and splinters flying into the air and Haupt had fallen to the ground. A ripple of fear went through his men but after a few seconds Haupt got up again, unharmed.

It was clear that it was not safe to stay where they were, so catching a rifle barrel held out to him for support and shouting to his men to follow him, Haupt too slithered down into the ditch. Finding Radtke already there with a number of men from different companies, Haupt,

The northern counterscarp gallery. Note the damaged railing along the top of the counterscarp and the gun embrasures. Radtke entered the ditch close to this gallery. Bundesarchiv Koblenz. Bild 1831/S2322

as the senior officer present, assumed command. To make it easier for the rest to follow him, he ordered some heavy timber that was lying nearby to be set up in the breach.

They had reached the ditch but to be safe from the shells the Germans had to get into the barracks. The iron door into the nearby counterscarp gallery was shut. One of the men chalked on it '5 Coy 24 IR' while others began to climb the earth rampart. Ahead of them, at the highest point of the fort, a *Musketier* of 5 Company was already waving a large red and yellow artillery flag in the hope of getting the artillery to lift their barrage. It had no effect. In the dusk and falling snow the artillery observers failed to see the signal and the shelling continued.

Into the barracks

Gritting their teeth, the men crawled on all fours up the steep slope from the ditch. The noise of the bombardment was so great that speech

German troops climbing down telegraph poles into the ditch. Possibly a reconstruction. Mémorial de Verdun

was impossible and orders had to be given by signs or by example. Approaching from the eastern side of the fort Radtke's group reached the *Rue du Rempart* without too much difficulty and got into the barracks through a doorway damaged by shellfire. Haupt's group, however, came from the north side and ran into violent fire from the machine guns in the tower of Douaumont church. Taking cover where they could, the men ran on across the top of the fort. At the *Rue du Rempart* a number of dark entrances were visible. To avoid the shells, Haupt and a small group of men fled inside.

After the noise of the bombardment the silence inside the barracks seemed menacing. With rifles and hand grenades at the ready, the Germans moved quietly forward. Suddenly, voices could be heard speaking French. Putting some broken French phrases together Lieutenant Klingenberg, 5 Company, ordered them to surrender. There was a silence. To keep down the tension, Haupt offered cigarettes round while they waited to see what would happen next. Then more Germans arrived, bringing with them a French gunner whom they had captured in an observation post. The gunner was ordered to persuade his comrades to surrender. Held fast by the coat tails, he led the Germans deeper into the labyrinth of the fort to where some twenty five of his comrades were sheltering on the lower floor. They included Warrant Officer Chenot, who the Germans were astonished to learn was in charge of the fort and who was visibly distressed to find that the fort had been captured by only a handful of the enemy. Then Radtke and his men appeared, having entered the barracks from a different direction. They rounded up other members

German troops lining up at the top of the ditch. Possibly a reconstruction.
Mémorial de Verdun

of the garrison and locked them in a barrack room.

With that the fort passed into German hands. Their astonishing success made the Germans fear that a hidden time bomb had been left behind to blow up the fort and Haupt now ordered Lieutenant Voigt to make a thorough search. Nothing suspicious was found but for safety's sake the French garrison was locked up in a room over the powder magazines for a couple of days before being taken away to Ornes and captivity.

By now many more Germans were arriving in the fort, among them twenty seven year old *Oberleutenant* Cordt von Brandis, a regular soldier who commanded 8 Company. At zero hour, 8 Company was on the extreme right of the 24th and still waiting for the 12th Grenadiers to come up. Impatient to be off, Brandis had waited for several minutes before deciding to advance with his right flank uncovered. Having rushed through the first French position on Hill 347, his company ran into heavy machine gun fire from Douaumont village that slowed them down for forty minutes and caused heavy casualties. When the 12th Grenadiers finally appeared, Brandis was at last able to hurry on towards the fort.

As they moved forward, Brandis met wounded coming back who told him that the fort was in German hands and that Haupt was dead.

Cordt von Brandis, third from the left, with his platoon commanders. The officer on the extreme left is Lieutenant von Eynatten (See Tour No. 4).
Bundesarchiv Koblenz. Bild 183/1987/0113/506

Meeting signallers on the road from Douaumont village to Bezonvaux at around 4.30pm, Brandis was able to send a telephone message to battalion headquarters to say that Fort Douaumont was firmly in German hands. He added that Haupt had been killed and that the artillery should lift its fire on the fort. As the news passed from battalion to division, however, it underwent a change. Not only did the message received by 6th Division state that the fort was firmly in the hands of *Oberleutenant* von Brandis but the request for the artillery to lift their fire had been lost along the way.

Brandis entered the fort with a small group of men from various companies almost one hour later than Radtke and Haupt. He also rounded up some prisoners and, meeting Haupt in the barrack block, they divided the task of organising the defence of the fort. Haupt took responsibility for internal security and Brandis, as second in seniority, was made responsible for external defence. A counter attack could be expected at any moment and, as darkness fell, French reconnaissance patrols coming up to the fort through driving snow were repulsed by brisk fire.

Major von Klüfer takes command

During the assault the commander of 2nd Battalion, Major von Klüfer, had been without any firm news of his scattered companies. At 4pm a sharp-eyed observer in a trench mortar battery had spotted a white flag on the glacis of the fort but no one had paid it any serious attention. A short while later, runners brought messages to say that the leading companies were immediately in front of the fort but it was almost 5.30pm before definite information was received by battalion headquarters. As luck would have it, the news came from Brandis, who after a brief stay in the fort had been sent back by Haupt. Shortly afterwards, signallers from 6 Company succeeded in making a telephone connection with the fort and Haupt confirmed that Fort Douaumont was indeed safely in German hands.

Authorizing Brandis to return to regimental headquarters to make a personal report on the events which had taken place, Klüfer set off with the remainder of the 2nd Battalion to take command of the fort.

The news that the fort had fallen to the 24th Infantry was received bitterly by the 12th Grenadiers. Arriving late in front of Douaumont village with their own right flank open, the 12th had met heavy fire and been unable to advance. Had they not had to wait for the 8th Leibgrenadiers to come up, the 12th argued bitterly, they could have gone on to storm the fort which by rights should have been their prize. Instead, the 24th had crossed into their sector and stolen the honour while the 12th fought to hold the right flank. Calmer thoughts prevailed when it became clear that it was their firm stand in the face of withering fire from the positions around the village that had enabled the 24th to go on. For many Grenadiers, however, the fact that without their exemplary courage and self-sacrifice the fort would have remained in French hands was small compensation for the bitter disappointment.

Douaumont ist gefallen!

The news that Fort Douaumont had fallen filled Germany with jubilation. Schools closed, church bells rang and everyone was filled with confidence. The official German communiqué, published at midday on 26th February, reported that:

> Fort Douaumont, the armoured northeastern pillar of the principal line of permanent fortifications of the fortress of Verdun, was taken by assault yesterday afternoon by the 24th Brandenburg Infantry Regiment and is firmly in German hands.

The French, however, tried to play down the disaster. The official French communiqué of the same day was a masterpiece of equivocation:

Front page of a special edition of the *Mecklenburgische Zeitung* reporting the fall of Fort Douaumont. H.P. von Müller's Estate

A fierce struggle is taking place around Fort Douaumont which is an advanced work of the old defences of Verdun. The position carried by the enemy this morning, after several fruitless assaults which involved them in very heavy losses, has been retaken and passed by our troops, which the best endeavours of the enemy cannot drive back.

When it became clear that there was no hope of recapturing the fort, French communiqués concentrated on the 'enormous losses' suffered by the Germans during repeated assaults on the fort and implied that its 'ruins' had only been occupied after a French withdrawal. But it was impossible to hide the truth for long and when the news finally came out, it was a devastating shock to the French. The reputation of Fort Douaumont was so great that many people could not believe it had been taken without a trick and the story that the German storm troops had been dressed in Zouave uniforms became widespread. No sufficient evidence to corroborate the story has ever come forward and for his part Chenot never sought to put the blame for its loss on a trick. As he said long after the war, had there been any 'false Zouaves' in Fort Douaumont, he would have seen them.

Aftermath

After so momentous an event it was clear that decorations would be awarded to the troops involved and two weeks after the fall of the fort a large number of Iron Crosses were sent up for distribution amongst those who had taken part in its capture. However, not everyone who had taken part was rewarded. Decorations were conferred on members of 7 and 8 Companies (including, according to one modern authority, even the cobblers, bakers and clerks) but 6 Company, all of whose officers had been killed or wounded, went empty handed, as did the pioneers. Inside the fort troops almost came to blows over the unfairness of the awards and only the constant threat from the enemy outside prevented serious trouble from breaking out.

The award of decorations to the main protagonists also caused trouble. It was Brandis who conveyed the news of the fort's capture back to regimental headquarters on 25 February and, on the basis of his account alone, brigade staff recorded that Fort Douaumont had been 'stormed by 7 and 8 Companies of the 24th led by *Hauptmann* Haupt and *Oberleutnant* von Brandis. Both officers most conspicuously distinguished'. On 28 February the divisional war diary mentioned both officers as 'equally deserving' of high distinction. Both were said to have 'broken through the defences of the fort at the same time and

A view of the ditch soon after the German capture of the fort. <small>Service Historique de l'Armée de Terre.</small>

in different places at the head of their storm troops, the impetus for the assault coming from them both at the same time and after mutual agreement'. As a result, Haupt and Brandis were awarded the *Pour le Mérite*, Germany's highest decoration, while Radtke, whose part in the events had been as great as Haupt's, was ignored.

When he realized the injustice that had taken place, Major von Klüfer tried to set the record straight but to no avail. Not only was his protest ignored but in a move amounting to a disciplinary sanction, Klüfer was sent back to the garrison at Neuruppin. Although some months later Radtke was awarded the Iron Cross 1st Class, his leading part in the storming of Fort Douaumont never received the reward it deserved. As the battle turned into bloody stalemate, the surprise capture of Fort Douaumont became in German minds a compensation for the taking of Verdun itself. Hindenburg called it 'a beacon of German heroism' and any correction of the legend surrounding its capture was impossible.

While Haupt slipped back into anonymity, Brandis became a hero and a favourite with the Crown Prince of Germany. His book, *Die Stürmer von Douaumont*, was an instant best seller and he was swamped with letters and offers of marriage. However, bitter quarrels over the injustice of the awards and decorations continued during the 1920s. During his lecture tours, Brandis was subject to catcalls and tumultuous scenes while Radtke's name was dropped from the list of former members of the 24th Infantry. It was when the Douaumont volume of *Schlachten des Weltkrieges* appeared in 1925 that Brandis's version of the capture of the fort was called into question. While being careful not to criticize Brandis directly and emphasizing the value of 8 Company's actions on the right flank, *Schlachten* made it plain that the war diaries had been drawn up on insufficient evidence and that the true leaders of the assault were Radtke and Haupt.

In 1934 Radtke produced his own book *(Douaumont wie es wirklich war)* and was belatedly rewarded with a painting of the Kaiser and promotion. Then Major von Klüfer produced his painstaking work on the subject and introduced into the picture a man previously unknown in the history of the capture of Fort Douaumont: Sergeant Kunze.

Kunze's story was an odd one. A twenty four year old regular sergeant from Thuringia, Kunze commanded a section of the 22nd Pioneers whose task was to accompany the first wave of storm troops and clear away any wire or other obstacle that might otherwise hold them up.

According to Kunze, having reached Strawberry Ravine without difficulty ahead of the first wave, he and his men got through a belt of wire and captured a French machine gun post. Reaching the road from Douaumont to Bezonvaux, they ran into machine gun fire from Douaumont church but Kunze pressed on boldly through the battered wire and reached the iron railing along the top of the ditch. Finding a breach on the eastern side of the fort, he got down into the ditch and then, using his men as a human pyramid, climbed into the northeastern counterscarp gallery through a gun embrasure.

Kunze then claimed that from the safety of the gallery he set off with two companions down the tunnel that led into the fort. There, he single-handedly captured the six-man crew of the 155mm gun turret but lost touch with his companions. Alone in the labyrinth of the fort he took a number of prisoners whom he locked up in a barrack room, before being distracted by the sight of fresh food and wine in a room reserved for officers. Having only had iron rations for several days, Kunze was overcome by hunger and he fell to, having first taken the precaution of getting one of his French captives to taste the food and make sure it was safe.

Neither Kunze nor Klüfer could ever satisfactorily explain why this story had lain hidden for so long. Lieutenant Voigt's report mentioned

Kunze as present in Fort Douaumont but at the time Kunze told no one about the 'storming' and no one else reported seeing him there. His story has never been officially disproved, although it has often been challenged on the ground that the events – and his long silence – are improbable. In the end, despite all the bitter disputes over the precise order of events, it is still impossible to say with absolute certainty who was the first German soldier to enter the barracks of Fort Douaumont on 25 February 1916.

Effect of the fall of Fort Douaumont

With the fall of Fort Douaumont, France lost the strongest and most modern of its defensive works at Verdun and the best observatory in the sector. It was the darkest hour of the whole assault and worse for French morale than the first four terrible days of the battle, which saw the destruction of an entire army corps and the loss of masses of artillery.

The effect on the battlefield was immediate. The commander of 37th (African) Division, the last of the units of XXX Corps still in the line, ordered the withdrawal of his troops to Belleville Ridge. Retreat to Belleville – which was the last of the ridges before Verdun - meant giving up all the forts and positions on the Right Bank and threatened the city itself. The bridge over the river at Bras was blown up and other bridges prepared for demolition. Seeing all these signs of imminent withdrawal, the civilian population of Verdun began to abandon the city but the French High Command remained firm. As guns, wounded and deserters poured back along the roads, Joffre ordered Pétain to hold the Right Bank of the Meuse at all costs. He had already threatened with court martial any commander who gave the order to retreat.

So the die was cast. The commanding position of Fort Douaumont was so important to the defence of the sector that the French had to retake it if the Right Bank was to be held. The Germans had to hold the fort if they were to continue their assault. For the next eight months the determination to hold or to retake Fort Douaumont, come what may, dominated the campaign at Verdun and drove both sides to the limits of endeavour, sacrifice and endurance.

Chapter Three

A TERRIBLE EXPLOSION

When night fell on 25 February the front formed a sharp salient. While Fort Douaumont and its immediate surroundings were in German hands, Douaumont village and Caillette Wood remained French.

The Germans expected the French to make an immediate attempt to retake the fort. Accordingly, during the night, the guard on the vulnerable south side was increased and ammunition, machine guns and reinforcements were brought up. Next morning, Voigt and a lieutenant from the 39th Field Artillery managed to bring the guns in the 75mm gun turret into action on French lines to the west and south of Douaumont village. Lieutenant Muller, whose 6 Company was responsible for the defence of the western perimeter, found French machine guns in cases in the fort and set them up in the northwestern machine gun turret, from where they threatened communication between the French rear and troops in the village.

Lieutenant Klingenberg, 5 Company, took over responsibility for internal security, which included guarding the prisoners and making arrangements to accommodate and feed the growing garrison. There were also wounded to be cared for – some eighty men from the 2nd and 3rd Battalions of the 24th Infantry had been injured in the assault - and in the days following the capture of the fort, an infirmary was set up on the lower floor.

As expected, on 26th February the French made an attempt to retake the fort. The operation was unsuccessful and in view of the extreme danger of the overall situation at Verdun General Pétain directed that, for the time being, plans to retake Fort Douaumont should be

Douaumont village after capture by the Germans in March 1916. H.P. von Müller's Estate

abandoned in favour of stabilizing the front. However, the remaining forts were to be regarrisoned, armed, supplied and ordered not to surrender even if entirely surrounded.

For the next eight months the forts provided the backbone of French resistance. It was around those in the central sector of the Right Bank – Douaumont, Vaux, Souville and Tavannes - that the high tide of the Battle of Verdun was to wash up and recede, leaving them like huge wrecks on a debris-strewn beach.

The Germans organise the fort

Having organised the immediate defence of Fort Douaumont, it became necessary to plan for its long-term occupation. The fort was allocated no permanent garrison but was defended by different units that rotated in and out at frequent intervals. They were recruited from among units serving in the sector, who regarded it as an honour to serve in the fort and to be called upon, if necessary, to defend it.

The incomparable possibilities for observation offered by the dominating geographical position of Fort Douaumont made it so important that an official artillery officer was appointed to it, who was directly responsible to the commandant. Under him were a dozen officers from various foot and field artillery regiments. As the Germans immediately discovered, from the relative safety of the eighty-centimetre wide steel observation domes, observers could look out over an area so extensive that it covered not only their own divisional and corps sectors but those of neighbouring army corps as well. More importantly, the domes – together with the observation post in the Bourges Casemate – also allowed the new German occupants of the fort to observe French movements on the whole of the Verdun front.

Part of the south side of the fort in April 1916. H.P. von Müller's Estate

The heavily damaged Bourges Casemate in 2001.

In addition to the observers, the garrison included signallers whose task was to ensure the vitally important communications with the rear. Since the thundering bombardment which the French had maintained on the fort since 25 February frequently cut the telephone lines, a parallel communication system was set up using acetylene lamps. Using the barrels of the 155mm and 75mm guns to concentrate the beams of light, coded messages were flashed from the gun turrets to receiving stations at Pillon, Hardaumont and Wavrille Wood. Light

Armoured observation post. Adapted from a German espionnage plan c.1911 in the collection of the Bibliothèque Municipale de Verdun. Scale 1:1000.

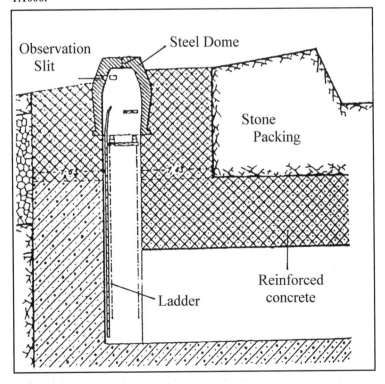

The entrance to the northeastern counterscarp gallery in 2001.

signalling was also possible from Ammunition Bunker VII and radio stations were set up in Bunker VI and the northwestern machine gun turret. In this way, artillery fire was controlled and directed, reinforcements requested, French troop movements reported and even, from time to time, personal messages sent and received.

The work of repairing and strengthening the fort was entrusted to pioneer units and an engineer officer was attached to the fort to oversee the work. His first task was to devise new, safe entrances and exits. Since the fort had been designed to meet an attack coming from the north and east, the main gateway was situated on the south side facing Verdun and from the day the fort fell to the Germans it naturally came under constant French bombardment.

New entrances were quickly made through the concrete wall of the northeastern counterscarp gallery and the double gallery at the northern apex of the fort. For troops leaving the fort for the front line, an exit was similarly made in the northwestern counterscarp gallery. Matters did not improve for long. The existence of these new gateways into the fort quickly became known to the French and they were subjected to increasingly intense bombardment. With well-aimed shells shrieking down night and day, getting safely in or out of the fort was a perilous undertaking, requiring not only strong nerves but a good deal of luck. The northeastern entrance was especially targeted by a field battery situated close to Fort Souville. With pounding hearts, men needing to enter or leave the fort crouched in trenches and shellholes outside or bunched up in the corridors inside, waiting for the right moment to make a dash for it. As soon as a salvo of shells had burst and before the showers of earth had settled, they leapt up and raced forward, hoping to make it to relative safety before the next shells fell.

Damage in the tunnel leading from the barracks to the exit in the northwestern counterscarp gallery. Jean-Luc Kaluzko

The demands of the front, the constant bombardment and the daily flow of men through the fort so hampered the work of improvement and repair that much was left undone. Nevertheless, during the weeks that followed its capture a number of steps were taken to make Fort

Barrack room inside Fort Douaumont. Bundesarchiv Koblenz.Bild 146/90/S5/29A

Douaumont a more effective strong point. Outside the fort, pioneer units laid telephone lines, constructed dugouts and trenches and laid out wire and other obstacles. Within the perimeter, infantry positions were constructed above the southern ditch, while the southern façade of the barracks was repaired and strengthened with sandbags. Close to the northern apex of the fort the pioneers constructed a ramp to permit the arrival of supplies and the evacuation of the wounded. Machine guns were installed in the Bourges Casemate and the counterscarp galleries. Trench mortars and flame throwers were brought up. Together with medical personnel, messengers and carrying parties, their specialized units formed part of the regular garrison of the fort.

The labyrinth of corridors and rooms inside Fort Douaumont provided the Germans with an invaluable refuge and depot in the immediate front line. The garrison was constantly augmented by troops passing through or taking shelter and while at first there was plenty of space, overcrowding soon became a problem. On average, one thousand troops passed through Fort Douaumont in each direction each night, although it was not unusual for there to be as many as three thousand men taking shelter in the only place in the sector where they could rest safely. In the confusion of ill-lit corridors, troops that had made the exhausting march up to the fort heavily laden with all types of necessary supplies crossed messengers, stretcher bearers, artillery observers, the wounded, the lost and those returning to the rear. All dropped their gear and snatched what rest they could on the floor, in corners, even on cases of ammunition, before braving the outside again.

Even though, once inside, troops were safe from the bombardment, Fort Douaumont was by no means a pleasant place to be. In the circumstances it was impossible to keep the fort clean. Rubbish of all sorts - stale food, excreta, used dressings, filthy uniforms – combined with hundreds of unwashed, lice-ridden, wounded, dying and dead men to produce a powerful stench. Ventilation was difficult because the French use of gas shells meant that openings to the outside had to be sandbagged. Paraffin lamps added carbon monoxide to the already foul air, so that oxygen equipment was kept available in such important parts of the fort as the infirmary and the commandant's quarters. Breathing difficulties, abscesses and headaches were common and fainting fits frequent, particularly when the weather was warm and still. The noise of the shelling rolling through the corridors made the barracks shake and shudder. Although the walls dripped with humidity, water was a great problem. When the Germans captured the fort, only two of the cisterns held water and that was insufficient for the needs of so many men. As a result, water had to be carried into the fort every day from the woods and ravines to the north. In the awful conditions men deteriorated visibly and some went mad. The artillery officer was relieved approximately every week but the observers were changed

Kitchen inside the fort. <small>H.P. von Müller's Estate</small>

Uses of the Barrack Rooms in Fort Douaumont

No.	Peace time occupation	German occupation	French occupation post-1916
1	Guard House	Destroyed	Destroyed
2 & 3	Guard Rooms	"	"
4	Administration	Operating theatre	Infirmary
5	"	Stretcher bearers	Garrison (infantry)
6	"	Seriously wounded	"
7	"	Doctor	NCOs
8	Siege headquarters	Walking wounded	Observation services
9	Engineer supplies	Food store	Blocked up
Passage between 8 & 9	Engineer supplies	Food store	Radio
10	Cistern	"	Food store
11 & 12	Cistern	Water barrel depot	Water storage
13	"	"	Repaired cistern
14	"	Pioneer depot	Machine room
15	"	"	Tool store
16	"	Depot	Ammunition, explosives
17-18	"	Depot	Weapons
19	"	Pioneer depot	Blocked up
20	Powder magazine	Orderly room	Engineer headquarters
21	"	Commandant's quarters	Commandant's quarters
Passage between 20 & 21	Powder magazine	Commandant's quarters	Telephone exchange
22-23	Commandant. Officers' kitchen	MG ammunition	Forge and workshop
Passage between 23 & 28	Commandant. Officers' kitchen	Cartridge magazine	Lamp room
24	Officers' quarters	Cartridge magazine (infantry)	Kitchen
Passage between 24 & 29	Officers' quarters	Cartridge magazine	Water filtration plant
25	Washing facilities	Destroyed	Destroyed
26	Other ranks kitchen and storeroom	Grenade depot	Engineer supplies
27	Emergency siege quarters	MG company	Temporary troops
28	"	Guard company (west)	Engineers, half company
29	"	"	Troop quarters
30	"	Reserve company, Left sector	Temporary troops
31	Troop quarters	Troops going up to the line	"
32	"	Weapons store	"
33	"	Equipment depot	Destroyed
34	Lamp room	Telephone exchange	MG blockhouse
35	NCO accountants	"	"
36	Troop quarters	Blocked up	Destroyed
37	"	Pioneer depot	Temporary troops
38	"	Destroyed	Floor destroyed
39 & 40	"	Motors etc }	
		Guard company (East)}	Temporary officers} and troops }
41	Bakery	Destroyed – machine guns	"
42	Infirmary	Pioneers	"
43	Artillery materiel	Machine guns	"
44	Woodworking shop	Façade destroyed, unusable	Blocked up, destroyed
45	"	"	Petrol dump
46	Troop latrines (wartime)	"	Troop latrines
47	Latrines (Officers)	-	Latrines (Officers)
48	Latrines (NCOs)	-	Latrines (NCOs)
49	Infantry ammunition	Artillery observers and Commandant's command post	Partly destroyed, used as a passage
50	Powder magazine	Officers	Office for temporary Troops
51 & 52	Powder magazine	"	Officers
53	"	"	Temporary officers
55	Bag cartridges – filling	Guard room	Petrol dump
56	"	"	"
I–II	Artillery Shelters	Victims of May explosion	German cemetery
III–IV–V	Artillery Shelters	Signallers and artillery observers	Passage
VI	Artillery ammunition depot	Radio station	Not cleared
VII	"	Light signalling station to Pillon	Destroyed

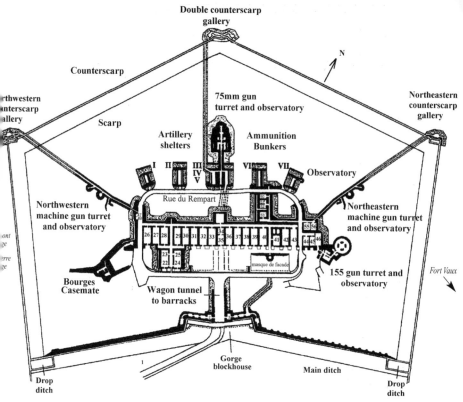

Plan of Fort Douaumont showing barrack rooms and main defensive features. Bibliotheque Municipale de Verdun. Scale 1:1000

Lower floor of Fort Douaumont. Bibliotheque Municipale de Verdun. Scale 1:1000

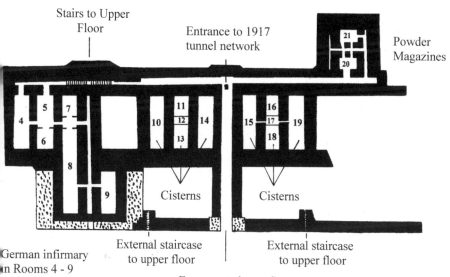

Former water cisterns, breached and used for other purposes.

more frequently, since service in such an exposed and cramped position under a constant bombardment was nerve-racking in the extreme.

In such a closed atmosphere the danger of an explosion or fire was ever present. Enormous amounts of ammunition of all types were stored in the fort, some of it in magazines but much of it simply stacked up wherever space could be found. The troops, grown careless of the danger and glad to be inside in relative safety, smoked, read, heated food and coffee, played cards and sat where they could, even on cases of explosive. Heavily armed with rifles, ammunition and grenades, they moved about the corridors, brushing against one another in the crowded and ill-lit passages.

In such conditions an accident was bound to occur sooner or later and it was during an offensive in early May, when the fort was especially crowded, that the inevitable happened.

The catastrophic explosion of 8 May

The War Diary of 5th Division records that on the evening of 7 May units of the 12th Grenadiers and the 52nd Infantry Regiment involved in the sector between Thiaumont Farm and the area to the south of Douaumont village had been relieved and had withdrawn to the fort. Seriously wounded survivors of the previous day's fighting filled the fort's infirmary to overflowing. Less seriously wounded and sick troops found what rest they could in the corridors, where they were joined by fresh men from the 8th Leibgrenadiers going up to support the operation planned for the following day.

At 6.10 am on 8 May, 5th Division received news of a serious explosion and fire in Fort Douaumont. Knowing how many men were in the barracks and fearing the worst, medical assistance and breathing apparatus was immediately dispatched to the fort, together with a company of pioneers. The artillery was ordered to be on the watch for an enemy attack which, to the surprise and relief of the Germans, never came.

Throughout the morning and afternoon a thick cloud of smoke hung over the fort, veiling, in the words of Werner Beumelburg, the author of the Douaumont volume of *Schlachten des Weltkrieges*, *'the fearful things that had happened underground'*.

The exact cause of the terrible explosion that occurred in the early hours of 8 May has never been established. The commonest speculation is that careless heating of coffee or food may have ignited the flame throwers, which were stored on the lower floor of the fort in the same area as a depot of hand grenades and the remaining French 155mm shells. Whatever the cause, at around 4.30am panic broke out in the fort. The fort's medical officer, Dr. Hallauer, 3rd Sanitäts-Kompanie, III Corps, who was on duty in the infirmary at that time, heard cries for help and terrified shouts of *Die Schwartzen kommen* (The blacks are coming). Before he could get help, three frightful explosions[1] shook the fort and all the lights went out. There was a terrible roar. A mighty blast ripped through the fort, blowing the doors in and shaking the infirmary. Hallauer was thrown back against the wall and stunned. When he staggered out into the corridor again he was met by a thick cloud of sulphurous smoke through which came cries and moans. Grabbing his gas mask, Hallauer opened the oxygen canisters and got the ventilator going. Stretcher-bearers helped him to carry some of the surgical patients out of the thick yellow smoke in the operating theatre and into another room where breathing was easier. Despite wearing his mask, Dr. Hallauer fainted. He was dragged away by two pioneers, who found him unconscious on the operating table. When he came round several hours later the full extent of the catastrophe met his appalled eyes.

The explosion had occurred in the southeastern sector of the fort on the lower corridor, where a large number of French 155mm shells were still stored. In this part of the corridor a hole two metres deep had been torn in the floor and had filled with water. Some metres further on, the roof had fallen in and debris blocked the corridor. The roof of the pioneer depot had been blown out. A massive stone staircase [2] had been ripped away by the blast and huge shell splinters were scattered in the rubble. In the main corridor relief troops from the 8th Leibgrenadiers - mostly young recruits - sat around, too stunned to move, while all around them lay other men, shocked, wounded and driven mad.

Dr. Hallauer's subsequent report to the commandant of the fort

Casualties of the terrible explosion. H.P. von Müller's Estate

showed the terrible extent of the catastrophe. The corridors were filled with rubble and bodies, some of them terribly mutilated. Arms, legs and torsos lay among smashed equipment. Many of the bodies were split open. In many places the dead were thrown on top of one another three or four deep. Against the end walls of some of the corridors on the lower floor smashed bodies were squashed together and heaped up and it was clear that the force of the explosion had travelled down the narrow corridors like a bullet from a gun and hurled them against the wall at the end. The bodies were without exception black and covered in gunpowder. Smoke and fumes filled almost all the corridors and barrack rooms, particularly on the lower floor. Some of the rooms were empty but in others the iron bedsteads had been hurled together into a heap, the bodies of their occupants catapulted out into the debris and rubble. Many of the dead were in a crouching position, some with their arms raised as if to protect themselves. In the rooms in which doors and beds were apparently little affected by the blast the dead were lying in bed as if asleep or sitting up wearing their gas masks.

Hallauer found hardly anyone who could help him with the injured. One doctor was dead and the others were either injured or too shocked to be of any use, as were nine of the stretcher bearers and nurses. Nevertheless, he managed with the help of men of the 8th Leibgrenadiers to bring a number of survivors outside and to clear some of the main corridors of the bodies filling them. Rescue work was hampered by the fact that to get from one side of the barracks to the other rescuers had to go outside into the ditch under fire. Later, help also came from units of the 24th Infantry in Caillette Wood and Brulé Ravine.

The German infirmary. Mémorial de Verdun

The room used by Dr. Hallauer as the main dressing station (2001). The brick wall was built after 1916. Jean-Luc Kaluzko

Some survivors did manage to totter out of the fort. In Hassoule Ravine to the northeast of the fort, Lieutenant Klingenberg saw men staggering towards him wearing German uniforms but without helmets or weapons. With faces and hands black with powder, singed hair and eyebrows and torn uniforms all they could do was stammer 'Douaumont...terrible'. Clouds of thick black smoke were rising from the fort. Fearing a successful assault by the French, Klingenberg ran towards the fort, noticing as he did so an entrance completely blocked by the bodies of men who had obviously fought with one another to get out into the fresh air. With other officers, he pulled away the sandbags protecting the barrack rooms on the gorge side of the fort and let fresh air flood in. As many men as possible were dragged outside but the lack of gas masks meant that it was a long time before all the rooms could be checked for injured and the blocked corridors cleared of wreckage and rubble.

The fact that the fort was so crowded meant that losses were exceptionally high. In the corridors and rooms near the centre of the explosion men were killed by the blast, suffocated by clouds of smoke, died under the rubble or were burned to death in the scorching heat. Several days after the explosion, the death toll was put at 679 identified officers and men and 1800 injured. Hallauer himself put the death toll at between 700 and 800 but admitted that the bodies were so mutilated as to make any proper identification impossible.

The frightfulness of it all left the survivors stunned. In the following days Hallauer noted, among other conditions, shock, confusion, agitation, loss of speech, convulsions and cases of raving madness. The fearful image of mass annihilation underground, the piles of mutilated corpses, the screams and groans of the wounded and the ravings of the insane had all raised the level of terror to unbearable heights. As Beumelburg wrote *'Es bleibt uns nur der hoffende Glaube, dass ein schnelles Vergehen die Furchbarkeit milderte'* (We can only hope that death came quickly to lessen the horror).

Fortunately for the rescuers, the French artillery, as if unaware of the magnitude of the explosion inside the fort and despite the thick clouds of smoke rising over it, remained fairly quiet, so the grim work of rescue and repair could go on undisturbed. The physical destruction inside the fort and the clouds of gas and smoke which filled the corridors and barrack rooms meant that it was some days before the 23rd Pioneers could get on with the awful work of dealing with the dead. Some of them were buried outside in an enormous crater left by the explosion of a 420mm shell but the task of taking all the hundreds of bodies outside was simply too much for the exhausted garrison. In addition, French shelling while the work was being carried out caused further losses. It was therefore decided to bury the dead in Artillery Shelters I and II on the *Rue du Rempart* and to wall up the entrances. Heavy shelling soon blocked access to the bunkers, leaving the vast majority of the victims of the explosion under tons of stones and rubble, where they still lie.

Dr. Hallauer's official report of 10 May attempted to reconstruct the

The northern exit from the barracks with Artillery Shelter No. 1 on the right. Bundesarchiv Koblenz. Bild 183/S 1796

events leading up to the explosion. Recalling a strong smell of flame thrower fuel in the fort on the previous day, he surmised, first, that an accident had ignited the inflammable oil and, second, that the resulting fire had given off thick clouds of smoke and soot. Some troops were burned and many others, their faces blackened with soot, ran in panic for the stairs and ladders to the upper floor. Seeing the black apparitions, German troops on the upper floor mistook them for black French soldiers and, fearing an attack, threw grenades at them. It was that, Hallauer believed, which may have caused the explosion of the French 155mm shells which, in turn, ignited a large store of hand grenades and detonators in the pioneer depot.

Terrible though it was, the explosion had no effect on the course of the battle. Within hours, specialist officers examined the fort to see whether it would continue to resist the French bombardment or whether it should be evacuated and blown up. Despite the magnitude of the blast, they found that Fort Douaumont was still worth holding. In fact, the physical damage suffered by the fort was far less serious than its effect on German morale. Until the explosion occurred, Fort Douaumont had been regarded as a safe haven for troops in the sector but news of the disaster on 8 May spread swiftly far and wide. From that moment on, in the minds of the German troops in the sector, the

Two victims of the May explosion lie in the German military cemetery at Mangiennes.

reassuring presence they affectionately referred to as 'the hill' really did become 'the coffin lid'.

Believing that a success in the field would lift morale, the commander of 5th Division, General Wichura, ordered the unsuccessful operation of 7 May in the area to the south of Douaumont village to be attempted again by the same regiments, even though they were worn out by the previous fighting and the explosion. The operation was fixed for 12 May. Despite vigorous artillery preparation and the use of gas, it was once again unsuccessful. A third attack using the same troops but without any artillery preparation was then ordered for the early hours of 13 May but it was called off before the exhausted German troops had time to show whether or not they could have carried it out.

Fort Douaumont's defences are strengthened

The explosion of 8 May caused major disruption to German operations in the sector. It also brought about a belated realization that the loss of the fort would have serious consequences. Fort Douaumont's importance as an observatory, command post, supply depot and reserve position were so overwhelming that its possession was indispensable to control of the sector north of Verdun. It was clear, however, that the German front line, which ran only a few hundred yards to the south, could scarcely be counted on to withstand the sort of artillery bombardment which would precede a French attempt to retake the fort. For its own safety, Fort Douaumont had to be able to resist an offensive by its own means. To do so artillery firepower would be needed, particularly if the fort was cut off. Unfortunately, by May 1916, the 75mm and 155mm gun turrets functioned as signalling stations and the Bourges Casemate housed machine guns. The counterscarp galleries were armed with a couple of elderly 121mm bronze cannon and a few 37mm revolver guns, of which only three were operational. Thus, the only artillery available to defend the fort was in the rear.

On 18 May all troops who were not needed in Fort Douaumont were ordered outside to make room for stores and supplies and to allow urgent defensive work to be carried out. Those permitted to remain inside were the commandant and his staff, the artillery officer with observers and the engineer officer with a company of pioneers. In addition, the garrison comprised two infantry companies, gunners, machine gunners, wireless and telephone operators and other specialist troops. The commanders of the two combat sectors held by 5th Division and one reserve company also remained in the fort, together with the medical service troops.

On 20 May, *Hauptmann* Kalau von Hofe, the newly appointed commander of the 1st Battalion, 12th Grenadiers, took over command of Fort Douaumont. At the time morale among the troops of 5th Division was very low. They had taken part in the attack on the fort in February, were in action again in March and, after a short period in Alsace, had returned to the Douaumont sector again towards the end of April. The explosion of 8 May and the unsuccessful offensives of 7 and 12 May had taken their toll, as had the endless supply difficulties connected with service in that sector. When, on 13 May, an Army Corps order instructed 5th Division to suspend offensive action it was received by the exhausted troops with relief. To lie quiet for a while and hold on to what had been gained seemed a good idea, provided the French would acquiesce.

But the French would not acquiesce. By the time *Hauptmann* Kalau von Hofe took over command there could be absolutely no doubt that a major assault on Fort Douaumont was imminent.

1. Some survivors speak of only two explosions
2. It is not clear to which staircase Dr. Hallauer refers. The stone staircase at the western end of the corridor is forty metres from the centre of the explosion and the staircase at the eastern end was wooden. Each cistern has a stone staircase at the entrance but they are at right angles to the centre of the explosion.

Chapter Four

A THUNDERSTORM OF SMOKE AND STEEL

By mid-May Douaumont did not look like a modern fort any more. The ruined and debris-filled ditches were no longer an obstacle. Three months of daily bombardment had torn gaping holes in the wide belts of wire and left the glacis and top of the fort a shapeless mass of interlocking craters. Although the barracks themselves remained intact, the constant shelling had cracked the roof and walls, bringing down stones and debris. Filled with tangled and discarded equipment of every kind and piled high with rubble, the corridors were unrecognizable and precise knowledge of them was needed in order to move around safely. A few candles burned here and there but during the shelling they were constantly blown out, leaving the troops in darkness. Some passages were deep in water, while others were so damaged that men had to bend double or crawl on hands and knees. The air was thick and the walls ran with foul, slimy water. Despite the difficult conditions the Germans worked constantly with whatever means came to hand to create and maintain shell proof access to the fort's vital organs, in particular the observation post in the Bourges Casemate and the radio station in the northwestern machine gun turret.

Yet, even damaged, the position of Fort Douaumont and its importance as an observatory, command post and reserve position were so overwhelming that possession of it was indispensable to control of the sector north of Verdun. The French were determined to retake it. Although General Pétain's first priority on taking over command at Verdun in February was stabilization of the front, he

German photo of the western ditch during 1916. Mémorial de Verdun

nevertheless followed General Joffre's instructions by ordering on 5 March that all Second Army operations should be ultimately directed towards the recapture of Fort Douaumont.

A definite plan to recapture Fort Douaumont began to take shape at the beginning of May, when General Pétain left Verdun to take over the Centre Group of Armies. On his departure, command of Second Army operations passed to General Nivelle, an attacking general who was determined to recapture the only fort in the sector that had fallen into German hands. The task of planning the operation was entrusted to another general well known for his aggressive qualities, Charles Mangin, commander of 5th Division.

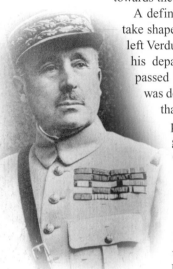

General Nivelle.
The Liberty Memorial Museum, Kansas City, Missouri.

A line of infantry entrenchments. The French needed to recapture positions like these at the top of Fausse-Côte Ravine.

Mangin's first plan proposed a wide operation along a three kilometre front. Before it could be implemented, however, a series of successful German operations pushed the French back from the fort. They also allowed the Germans to seize two important ravines: Fausse-Côte Ravine on the southeastern side of Fort Douaumont and Couleuvre Ravine on the western side. In a subsequent operation the Germans seized the high ridge to the south of Couleuvre Ravine and occupied the important French positions along it. These ravines provided the Germans with natural access routes for a counter attack if the French assaulted the fort and the ridge gave them extended visibility towards French lines to the south and southwest.

Mangin knew that it would be dangerous to try to retake Fort Douaumont as long as the Germans held those positions. His second plan therefore proposed that any attempt to do so should be preceded by an operation to seize the former French positions at the top of the two ravines in order to block any German advance on the fort by that route. The success of the

76

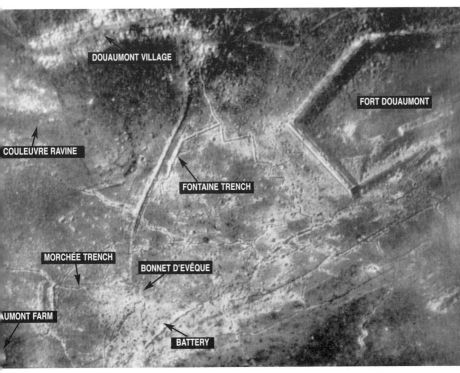

DOUAUMONT VILLAGE

FORT DOUAUMONT

COULEUVRE RAVINE

FONTAINE TRENCH

MORCHÉE TRENCH

BONNET D'EVÊQUE

UMONT FARM

BATTERY

Aerial photo of the sector to the west of Fort Douaumont. Note shelling around the road junction. The French 36th Infantry suffered heavy casualties in this area. H.P. von Müller's Estate

plan depended not only on taking those positions but also on having the necessary means to seize and hold the objectives.

Accordingly, Mangin asked for four divisions, but his request was refused. A further request for two divisions in line and a third in reserve was also refused. By May 1916 the French High Command was preparing the coming Somme offensive and Joffre was determined to keep the maximum resources available for his own use. He made it clear that no further divisions would be forthcoming and Pétain had no choice but to accept the situation. Mangin was finally allocated one division for the assault and one in reserve, which he considered far from sufficient. In Mangin's view, preparation of the necessary communication and jump-off trenches would alone have required a whole division.

Faced with the shortage of resources, General Nivelle reduced the scope of the operation. The final plan published on 13 May fixed the objectives of the assault as Morchée Trench, Bonnet-d'Evèque (a strong position situated between Thiaumont Farm and the fort), Fontaine Trench, Fort Douaumont, the machine gun turret to the east of the fort and Hongrois Trench. If successful, the operation would form a salient 500 metres deep and 1150 metres wide at the base.

The plan of attack

General Mangin.
The Liberty Memorial Museum, Kansas City, Missouri.

The operation was fixed for 22 May. It was to be carried out by III Corps (General Lebrun) using Mangin's 5th Division – by coincidence facing the German 5th Division – 71 Brigade, three balloon companies and one fighter group. The main thrust was to be led by two battalions of the 129th Infantry Regiment, each supported by one pioneer company and two machine gun companies. The 2nd Battalion (*Commandant* Maguin) was to attack the fort directly from the south, sending 6 Company around the eastern side of the ditch. The 1st Battalion (*Commandant* Vaginay) was to advance along the western side of the fort to a point close to the northern apex, taking Fontaine Trench and linking up with 6 Company. At the same time, two battalions of the 74th Infantry Regiment would attack along the eastern and southeastern sides of the fort and seize certain vital positions, including the machine gun turret on the ridge to the east.

The operation was to be supported on the right flank by one company of the 274th Infantry and on the left flank by a battalion of the 36th Infantry. At the same time, diversionary attacks were to be carried out by neighbouring units in front of Fort Vaux and on the north side of Dame Ravine. True to character, Mangin specifically ordered that any ground taken was to be held at all costs and not given up without orders.

Preparation of the ground for the assault required the construction of almost twelve kilometres of trenches as well as the creation of depots, stores and medical facilities that under normal circumstances would have taken six weeks. The assigned pioneer and territorial companies went to work at once but their numbers were insufficient and, in the short nights, little was achieved. To make matters worse, from French prisoners taken on 13 May the Germans learned the details of the impending attack. They immediately ordered a counter barrage that destroyed the work so painstakingly carried out as fast as it was completed and caused such serious losses that the successful preparation of jump-off trenches was limited to sectors out of sight of the enemy.

For the month before the operation 5th Division was in rest. Infantry officers paid extensive visits to Forts Landrecourt and Moulainville while pioneer officers received special briefings on Fort Douaumont. To raise morale, parades were held at which stirring speeches were given and on 15 May Mangin proudly decorated his regiments with the Croix de Guerre. By 21 May all units were in place. Expecting a success, *Commandant* Maguin, was appointed commander of Fort Douaumont even before the operation began.

French artillery preparation begins

When the French bombardment accelerated on 17 May, Fort Douaumont disappeared behind a curtain of smoke and fire. The noise was so great that it was only by shouting directly into his neighbour's ear that a man could make himself heard. On 21 May, Colonel Estienne, the artillery commander, sent word to General Mangin that Fort Douaumont was as full of holes as a sieve. Mangin confidently told his officers that they would be able to advance with rifles slung because the fort would be 'completely destroyed'. Events were to prove otherwise.

Fully effective or not, for the Germans crammed together inside Fort Douaumont the French 'softening-up' operation was a period of intense suffering. For five days the heavy shells rained down and little

Barrack room inside Fort Douaumont. Bundesarchiv Koblenz. Bild 146/90/S5/29A

by little the fort began to crumble. From the top of the fort the fountains of smoke and earth hurled up by the heavy calibre French guns rose vertically into the air and fragments of the roof fell down on the men crouched inside. Conditions soon became unbearable. Shells falling on the southern façade and the main entrance blew huge holes in the walls and threw stones and splinters far into the corridors with an ear-splitting din. Men caught in the blast were blown along the corridor or flung against the wall. Gradually the barrack rooms and corridors filled with cement-laden dust and breathing became difficult. Exhaust gases from an electricity generator installed on 20 May spread throughout the inside of the fort, filling the corridors with a poisonous stench. The constant feeling of nausea brought on by the choking mixture of chlorine, tobacco, sweat and foul latrines was soon made worse by the indescribable horror of the decomposing bodies previously buried in the southern ditch and now disinterred by the shelling. Water supplies began to run out and vermin flourished. As the days passed, the tunnel between the barracks and the main entrance collapsed and the principal ground floor corridor became blocked with debris. Pioneers worked tirelessly at repairing the damage but the air grew thicker and casualties increased, adding to the burden on the medical staff who were already fully occupied in treating and evacuating the wounded, filtering the drinking water and keeping the infirmary ventilated.

Entrance tunnel to the Bourges Casemate in 2001.

Until 20 May, however, Fort Douaumont still functioned as an observatory and reinforcements continued to arrive. In the gun turrets the artillery observers carried on their work to the point of complete exhaustion. During the afternoon of 20 May a series of heavy shells crushed the tunnel leading to the Bourges Casemate, cutting it off from the rest of the fort. As an observation post and a link with the front lines to the south of the fort, the Bourges Casemate was vital so a company of pioneers

80

was immediately sent to re-establish access. Here, at least, the occupants were found alive. The radio operators in the northwestern machine gun turret were not so lucky. At almost the same moment as the Bourges Casemate was cut off, a shell struck the tunnel leading to the radio station and the post went up in flames.

On 22 May the rain of fire rose to unprecedented levels. The tunnel to the Bourges Casemate collapsed repeatedly and a direct hit blocked access to the 75mm turret. By now, both radio stations were destroyed. During the day the last remaining observation post - the armoured dome serving the 155mm turret - was swallowed up under heaps of rubble while inside the barracks a direct hit blew a whole barricade of sandbags onto the generator, putting out all the lights. One by one the corridors fell in. On the highest alert but quite unable to see what was happening outside, the German garrison huddled silently together, waiting for the assault.

If conditions were bad inside Fort Douaumont, for the German troops in the front line the five days of artillery preparation were pure hell. On 18 May, French harassing fire struck them like a thunderstorm of smoke and steel. In a matter of hours the positions so painfully constructed during the long winter nights had totally disappeared and all that could be seen of the fort were huge plumes of smoke. Losing sight of their comrades, men desperately sought protection in shell holes or folds in the ground. The next day the bombardment increased. Like a giant plough working remorselessly back and forward, the shells turned the earth over and hurled it up into the sky. Great clouds of gas spread as far as the fort. Rations and water ran out; runners and casualties disappeared without trace. Soon, all communication between the front lines and the fort was lost and although during the night pioneers strove desperately to restore it, their work was destroyed the moment dawn broke. When zero hour came on 22 May, there was little left of the 8th Leibgrenadiers and 52nd Infantry who had held the lines in front of the fort. The only survivors of the 52nd were a tiny group still fighting on the German right flank towards Thiaumont Farm. The three companies of Leibgrenadiers had been reduced to three officers and thirty four men.

22 May: The French jump off

The French artillery preparation had not, however, managed to silence the German counter barrage and in their half-completed trenches the French infantry suffered heavily. In an attempt to silence the German artillery, French planes attacked eight observation

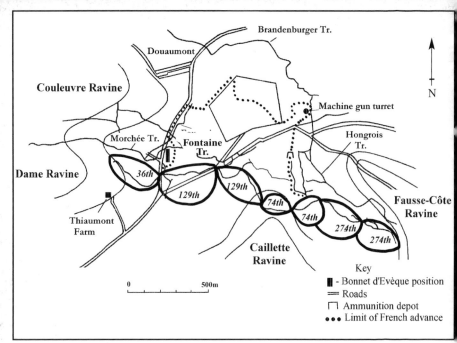

The French attack on Fort Douaumont, 22 May 1916. Adapted from *Les Armées Françaises dans la Grande Guerre*, Tome IV, Vol. 2.

balloons early on 22 May and, for good measure, also bombed the Crown Prince's headquarters in Stenay. Shooting down six of the balloons put most of the German air observation out of action but neither operation prevented increased shelling of the French front lines later in the morning. A violent German barrage twenty minutes before zero hour caused such serious casualties in French ranks that *Commandant* Maguin asked for reinforcements. By the time the operation began, the five companies available to Maguin had been reduced to an average of forty five men and 7 Company had lost all its officers. Nevertheless, at 11.50 am the four assault battalions formed up as well as they could in the shattered terrain and, in brilliant sunshine, jumped off behind a rolling barrage provided by 75mm field guns.

On the extreme left of the operation the 36th Infantry quickly seized Morchée Trench and Bonnet-d'Evêque but suffered heavy casualties and could not advance further. On the extreme right, the 274th Infantry was pinned down by violent fire and the only company that managed to jump off disappeared completely. In Caillette Wood, the 74th Infantry met such intense resistance that one battalion was unable to leave the trenches. The other, led by *Commandant* Lefebvre-Dibon, succeeded in achieving its objectives – the ammunition depot and

82

DUAUMONT VILLAGE

EST TRENCH

75mm GUN TURRET

EASTERN MACHINE GUN
TURRET AND BATTERY

BOURGES CASEMATE

ENTRANCE BLOCKHOUSE

COMBAT SHELDTER DV1

DEPOT

INFANTRY
ENTRENCHMENTS

CAILLETTE WOOD

Aerial view of Fort Douaumont and surroundings, April 1915. H.P. von Müller's Estate

Combat Shelter DV1 at the edge of Caillette Wood and the machine gun turret to the east of the fort – only to find itself unsupported. Alone and under threat of attack from three sides, the battalion commander set up his command post in the partly demolished depot, barricading the entrance, clearing out the dead and trying as best he could to help the wounded who continued to flood in.

In the centre of the operation, however, initial progress was rapid. Vaginay's battalion went beyond its objectives in only a few minutes, seizing Fontaine Trench and taking up positions close to the northern apex of the fort. Also meeting little resistance, Maguin's battalion easily took the trenches on the southern side of the fort before hurrying on up the glacis. After months of bombardment the ditch was no longer the obstacle that it had been in February and the first units got quickly into the fort through breaches on its western and southern sides. Once inside the perimeter the troops – by this time, pioneer and infantry units had become mixed – turned in different directions, some making for the counterscarp galleries, others heading for the main entrance or spreading out towards the gun turrets and the barracks.

The northeastern and eastern sides of the fort posed a serious problem for 6 Company. Even before jumping off, that unit had suffered serious casualties when the captain and all his staff were killed in the assault trenches. Attempting now to advance along the eastern side of the fort, the small group of survivors was caught in violent machine gun fire and flung back into the southeastern ditch. A short while later a support company attempted to move forward and fill the gap but they too were unable to advance. That left the eastern side of Fort Douaumont unoccupied by the French.

Over on the western side, however, troops from 5 Company rapidly took the Bourges Casemate by means of a bold rifle and grenade attack through the gun embrasures. They then seized the damaged counterscarp gallery at the northwestern corner of the fort before moving on to the double gallery at the northern apex. Left to organise the conquered positions, a pioneer unit tried to explore the tunnel between the counterscarp gallery and the barracks but found it blocked. They returned to the Bourges Casemate, where the tunnel was open. The pioneers followed it to the end. Hearing German voices and seeing a machine gun installed behind a barricade, the pioneers retreated, building their own barricade and making a loophole through which to fire at any Germans who might approach.

While 5 Company was dealing with the gun positions, 8 Company was attempting to carry out its orders to occupy the superstructure, seize the main entrance and clear the barracks. Arriving in the ditch on the southwestern side, 8 Company divided into two columns. The first headed up the steep earth slope onto the superstructure to deal with the gun positions, while the second pushed along the ditch towards the main entrance. There, they met heavy fire and were unable to advance.

The northeastern machine gun turret today.

Hand grenades thrown at the façade of the blockhouses simply bounced off and were more dangerous to the attackers than the defenders. The French were later driven out of the southern ditch and onto the glacis, where they dug in and fought valiantly to repel German counter attacks out of the main entrance.

On the superstructure, brisk fire from the northeastern machine gun turret caused heavy casualties but did not prevent the French from taking the northwestern turret, which was seriously damaged. They soon found, however, that the passage leading from the turret into the barracks was blocked with debris, making access impossible. A grenade attack on the outside of the 75mm turret was unsuccessful and because the French wished to capture the turret in working order, no demolition charges were laid. In fact, although the French did not know it, the German signallers inside the turret continued sending light signals down the gun barrels throughout the assault, informing headquarters of the situation and requesting reinforcements. Pressure on the signallers was so intense that they changed every fifteen minutes. They later reported that they fully expected the French to put a stop to the communication at any moment by pushing clods of earth into the gun barrels.

Having failed to gain access to the barracks from the gun positions and the main entrance, the French looked for other means of getting inside. All the openings into the southern side were blocked with sandbags and the shell torn entrance at the western end of the barracks was strongly defended by grenades and machine gun fire. Unable to advance, a group of pioneers began to dig a trench between the barracks and the Bourges Casemate, covering the western entrance and preventing the Germans from breaking out towards the south.

One hour had now passed and losses had been so great that it was already clear to the French troops involved in the operation that,

85

The western entrance to the barracks, with the Bourges Casemate on the left. French pioneers dug a trench between the two to prevent the Germans from breaking out. H.P. von Müller's Estate

without reinforcements, they would never retake Fort Douaumont. A company of the 36th Infantry was promptly sent up but a sharp German bombardment as they were crossing the ditch caused heavy casualties. Linking up with the survivors of 8 Company, the remnants of the 36th hastily set off over the chaotic terrain to clear the top of the fort. They were soon thwarted by violent machine gun fire and many officers and men were killed, including 8 Company's commander, Lieutenant Guéneau de Mussy. Grabbing their entrenching tools, the remainder started to dig in.

Within a few minutes of the start of the attack, *Commandant* Maguin sent news to headquarters that men of the 2nd Battalion could be seen on top of Fort Douaumont. Aerial observation later confirmed that the French covered approximately two thirds of the surface of the

Under the cupola of the 75mm gun turret.

fort from a point just west of the northern apex to the southeastern corner. To the delighted French command it seemed as if success was within their grasp. However, the Germans still controlled the eastern and northeastern sides of the fort, including the armoured 75mm and 155mm turrets and the northeastern machine gun turret. Moreover, the vast majority of the fort's defenders were safe inside the barracks, where they were protected from the annihilating bombardment that the Germans now unleashed in an attempt to stop the assault.

Die Franzosen sind da!

The sudden appearance of French troops on the south side of the barracks caused some panic among the defenders of Fort Douaumont but it was quickly quelled by the commandant, Hauptmann Kalau von Hofe. As the first troops came into sight he ordered machine guns to be set up at each end of the wagon road that ran through the western end of the barracks. Trench mortars were hurriedly dug out of the rubble to protect the southwestern side of the fort. The Leibgrenadiers rushed along to the eastern end of the main block and hurried up the earth massif opposite the entrance where, supported by Grenadiers standing shoulder to shoulder in the ruined southern side of the barracks, they poured devastating fire onto the approaching attackers. Others took up positions on the eastern side of the fort with the aim of preventing French troops on the nearby ridge from linking up with those to the south or, from the roof of the barracks, pinned down the French arriving from the southwest. A group of six men detailed to defend the double counterscarp gallery in the fort's northern apex rushed off along the underground tunnel and, finding that the gallery was already in French hands, blocked the tunnel with a barricade of sandbags. Ignoring invitations to surrender, they waited until a party of volunteers from inside the fort took the French from the rear. The sandbag barricade was later demolished and a company of Grenadiers took up positions in the gallery to make sure it was not taken again.

In the nearby 75mm turret the signallers worked frantically to send out messages. The smoke and fumes from the French bombardment to the north of the fort were so thick that at first nothing could get through. It was almost 1.30 pm before the receiving station at Wavrille picked up a desperate request for reinforcements. A counter attack was immediately ordered but the troops coming up from Hassoule Ravine through the French bombardment suffered heavy casualties. It was late in the evening before fresh troops managed to arrive.

Even though the French had not managed to get inside the barracks,

The battered Bourges Casemate in 2001 with, on the right, the western entrance to the barracks. The machine gun nest was on top of the Bourges Casemate.

their control of a large area of the superstructure was a serious blow to the Germans. From positions on the roof the French could hurl grenades down on attempts to counter attack out of the western end of the barracks. A well-protected machine gun nest quickly installed on top of the Bourges Casemate by units of the 34th Infantry devastated repeated German attempts to break out to the south. Attempts to smoke the French out of the casemate were unsuccessful and throughout the night and the next day it remained a serious obstacle to German attempts to re-establish control over the fort.

By nightfall French ranks on the fort were seriously depleted. Despite that, they managed to hold off several German counter attacks and even established communication with other French troops who were dug in on the northwestern glacis. A few reinforcements dribbled in during the evening and at midnight Maguin sent up a case of grenades. But the Germans were still holding the barracks and the northeastern side of the superstructure and were well dug in between the main entrance and the eastern corner of the ditch. More importantly – and disastrously for the French – the entrance to the barracks through the double gallery at the northern apex of the ditch and the northeastern corner were still in German hands and enabled them throughout the operation to bring up reinforcements and supplies.

23 May

The Germans reinforced Fort Douaumont during the night while the pioneers worked tirelessly to construct barricades and defences. Unaware that there were Germans on the superstructure, a few German batteries continued to fire on the fort causing considerable losses among their own men and adding to the injured in the over-crowded infirmary. It took seven consecutive messages from the signallers in the 75mm turret before the batteries held their fire.

Inside the fort, the commandant and his staff were considering possible plans for saving Fort Douaumont from recapture. During the night divisional orders had been received instructing the Germans at all costs to launch an attack from the fort towards the south. Before they could do so, however, the French attacked again, strongly supported by the machine guns on top of the Bourges Casemate. During the ensuing fight the French were forced to take cover but the Germans also suffered greatly. Taken in the rear by the French machine guns and once again hit by their own field artillery, the Germans suffered heavy losses and pulled back inside the fort.

Then a strange sight presented itself to the defenders of Fort Douaumont. An order from General Wichura insisting on an all out attack towards the south was brought to the fort in person by a captain of the Ziethen Hussars accompanied by two lieutenants. Resplendent in fresh, clean uniforms, each of them armed only with a gas mask and a stick, they formed a striking contrast to the exhausted and filthy defenders of the fort. The pristine Hussars were advised that by the time General Wichura's message arrived, two unsuccessful attempts to break out to the south had already been made. At dawn, a company of Jägers trying to make a sortie out of the western entrance had been stopped by a flurry of grenades from French troops on the roof. Later, a party of seventy Grenadiers that had come up to Fort Douaumont during the night had attempted to launch an attack on the casemate from the eastern end of the barracks but it too had fallen a prey to the machine guns. Attempts made during the day to reach the casemate through the underground passage from the fort were also unsuccessful.

To implement General Wichura's order, a third attempt to break out was now undertaken. Once again, the Germans were cut down by the French machine guns in their rear, although this time some of them

French machine guns prevented German attempts to break out.

managed to reach the top of the ditch. For a while it looked as if the break-out would be successful but German shells falling short once again broke up the attack and, unable to return to the fort, the surviving German troops took shelter where they could. It was midnight before reinforcements succeeded in reaching them.

On the basis of reports received on 22 May the French High Command had announced that Fort Douaumont had been captured. They now ordered further troops to be sent up 'to clear the barracks of the few Germans who might still be there'. Approaching the fort over 600 metres of shell-torn ground in broad daylight and in full view of the enemy batteries and machine guns, the 200-strong unit was reduced to an officer and forty men before they reached the glacis. On reaching the superstructure, a glance around was enough to convince the captain that the situation was very different from what he had been led to believe. Almost twenty four hours after the start of the operation, the French were nowhere near to occupying the fort and the situation was becoming hourly more unfavourable. The fact that the Germans had retained control of the barracks meant that the defenders were safe inside while the French were outside at the mercy of the German bombardment, which now rose to new heights, presaging a counter attack.

It soon came. During the afternoon, the exhausted 74th Infantry was encircled and forced to surrender the machine gun turret to the east of the fort, as well as the depot and the combat shelter at the edge of Caillette Wood, positions which they had held against desperate odds for twenty five hours, taking over 72% casualties. On the fort itself casualties were extremely high as the last shreds of the 129th were withdrawn during the night. By then, all that remained in French hands were the northwestern machine gun turret and counterscarp gallery, the western side of the superstructure, the western ditch and parts of the southern ditch. To the ragged survivors that held them it was by now perfectly clear that the operation to retake Fort Douaumont would be unsuccessful.

General Mangin ordered 5th Division to be relieved after first re-

Former machine gun turret and 74th Infantry monument on the ridge to the east of Fort Douaumont.

establishing the situation to the right and left of the fort. Carried out at dawn on 24 May without artillery preparation, the attempt to re-establish the situation on the right ended in bloody failure. The attack on the left was postponed in the face of the aggressive spirit shown by the Germans along the whole front.

24 May: the end of the offensive

By dawn on 24 May the Germans had drawn up a detailed plan to deal once and for all with the Bourges Casemate. Under cover of darkness a heavy trench mortar was manhandled into position in the southern ditch less than eighty yards from the machine gun nest but out of the direct line of fire. In quick succession, eight shells were hurled at the casemate and, as the last one fell, the commandant himself led three companies out of the fort to fall on the shattered defenders who, stunned and exhausted, gave themselves up. The prize was seven machine guns, five of them completely destroyed, and 170 men of the 34th Infantry Regiment.

Little by little, the fort was cleared of French troops. In all, sixteen officers and 500 men were taken prisoner and a large number of machine guns captured. Later in the day, a strong force of fresh Bavarian troops who had come up during the night attacked in force at the northwestern angle and on the southern flank, encircling the fort and pushing the French back to their original positions.

The first French attempt to retake Fort Douaumont had ended in failure. Of 5th Division there was not even one company left in reserve and when General Lebrun ordered Mangin to attack again immediately, he refused and was relieved of his command. However, the operation had been costly for both sides. According to *Schlachten des Weltkrieges* – which gives no final figure – casualties among the 52nd Infantry, 12th Grenadiers and 8th Leibgrenadiers amounted to approximately 4,500 men when they were withdrawn on 28 May. French losses in 5th Division for the period between 18 and 27 May were 5,640 killed, wounded and missing. Despite the casualties, the French Commander-in-Chief, General Joffre, sent General Nivelle a congratulatory telegram expressing satisfaction at the magnificent effort made by the Second Army. In fact, as far as the French High Command was concerned, the offensive

91

Fort Moulainville. The commander warned Mangin that he would not succeed in retaking Fort Douaumont without heavier artillery.

had not been entirely in vain; it had raised Second Army morale and proved to the Germans that the French were still determined to take the initiative. Moreover, it had obliged the Germans to make use of troops intended for a major operation on the Right Bank.

Mangin's official report of 30 May identified several reasons for the failure. The narrowness of the front had allowed the Germans to concentrate their efforts on a very small area. The reserves were insufficient, too far back and, coming from a quiet sector, were unprepared for the terrible conditions at Verdun. The artillery had not succeeded in suppressing German counter battery fire and had been insufficient to destroy the fort. Mangin had, in fact, been warned by the commander of Fort Moulainville – which had survived daily bombardment by German 420mm mortars since the start of the Battle of Verdun – that the artillery available to him would be insufficient to crack the concrete carapace of Fort Douaumont. No such heavy artillery being available to the French at the time, Mangin had no alternative but to proceed without it.

There were also other reasons for the failure. Important points such as German reserve positions and observatories escaped the preliminary bombardment. The French failure to encircle the fort left the eastern side unoccupied, which allowed the Germans to bring up supplies and reinforcements even while under attack. Communication and jump-off trenches were insufficiently prepared and nothing had been done to improve communications between the French forward positions in Caillette Wood and Mangin's headquarters at Fort Souville.

Licking their wounds, the French now went back on the defensive. Inside the fort, however, the new commandant, Major Schemmel, 20th Bavarian Infantry, received a long overdue order: Fort Douaumont was to be made an impregnable stronghold.

Chapter Five

THE STRONGHOLD RETAKEN

The fearful artillery battle that had accompanied the French offensive in May had reduced Fort Douaumont to a heap of concrete surrounded by a sea of stinking mud. Mounds of rubble and gigantic shell holes encumbered access to the barracks which, where they were

Aerial view of Fort Douaumont during the summer of 1916. Mémorial de Verdun

not destroyed, were in total disorder. With telephone lines cut and radio stations out of order, signal lamps alone maintained communication between the fort and the outside world.

In order to relieve pressure on the fort, the Germans strove during the summer to push the front on the Right Bank as far to the south as possible. At the end of May, a massive offensive was launched with the intention of punching a hole in French lines and seizing four bases for a final assault on Verdun. Three of these bases – the Thiaumont ouvrage, Fleury village and Fort Souville – lay along Fleury Ridge, the last of the major cross-ridges before Verdun and the final line of resistance for the city. Behind Fleury lay only Belleville Ridge, whose two secondary forts were not considered capable of offering any serious resistance. The fourth base was Fort Vaux, which buttressed the northeastern sector of the French line.

On 2 June the Germans succeeded in occupying the superstructure of Fort Vaux, although it took a further five days to subdue the garrison. On 23 June the Germans hurled 70,000 men along the line between Thiaumont and Fort Vaux, drenching the French with a new sort of gas – phosgene – against which their masks offered no protection. The French managed to slow down the German advance by several hours but could not prevent them from finally seizing Thiaumont and Fleury village. Then, on 1 July, the launch of the long-awaited Somme offensive by British and French troops forced the Germans to meet a second major operation on the Western Front. On 11 July, in a last desperate attempt to break through to Verdun, they threw 40,000 men into the attack along a line from Fleury to the eastern edge of the battlefield. They gained a temporary footing on

The towers of Verdun cathedral, a mere five kilometres from Fort Souville.

Fort Souville but were unable to take the fort itself. In bitter fighting, Fleury and the Thiaumont ouvrage changed hands many times before Fleury was retaken on 18 August. Finally becoming impatient with the lack of success at Verdun, on 28 August the Kaiser ordered the Chief of the German General Staff, Erich von Falkenhayn, to be replaced by Field Marshal von Hindenburg. Promptly declaring Verdun to be a running sore, Hindenburg ordered the cessation of all attacks.

Inside Fort Douaumont

Among the papers found on a French staff officer captured on 22 May were precise plans of Fort Douaumont. Using them, the German pioneers set systematically to work to make the fort impregnable. Their efforts were constantly disrupted by the flow of troops and wounded through the fort and the mounds of supplies and materiel that piled up in the passageways and barrack rooms. Realizing that Fort Douaumont could not be properly defended as long as it remained in so chaotic a state, the commandant set out to organise life inside as if it were a barracks in peacetime.

The officer on the left is Hauptmann Frentzen, Engineer Officer attached to the fort from May to October 1916. He was responsible for the defensive improvements to the fort. H.P. von Müller's Estate

The highest priority was the Herculean task of cleaning the fort of all the filth that had accumulated during May. In addition to soiled bandages and dressings, discarded and stained uniforms, rotten food and every type of equipment – not to mention ammunition and explosives in such quantities that a newly-arrived artillery officer compared it to sitting on a volcano – there were bodies to dispose of. The dead of the previous few weeks had not been buried but had simply piled up in half empty ammunition depots, where, in the warm spring air, they had begun to decompose. So awful was the task of cleaning the fort that breathing apparatus was sometimes required. The collected refuse was dumped two kilometers away from the fort, as were the remaining live French 155mm shells, each one of which had to be carried out of the fort at night, with the ever-present French bombardment offering the possibility of instant annihilation. As for the human remains, volunteers carried them outside for burial but, even so, a smell of corpses hung in the air for weeks afterwards.

Within a month, the stinking chaos inside Fort Douaumont had been replaced by cleanliness, order and routine and a programme of defensive improvements could begin. Supplying the necessary materials presented great difficulty. In the darkness it was not easy to find a safe passage across the chaotic terrain and braving the belt of fire around the fort was enough to test the courage of any man. Every night, troops laden like donkeys toiled up from the depots in the rear, weighed down by loads of wood or iron. Those materials that were not dropped or lost on the way – a report drawn up in September described the flanks of Fort Douaumont as covered with 'an innumerable quantity of useful objects' – had to be shared between the fort and the front line. As the front line often took priority, work planned for the fort was neglected.

Nevertheless, some progress was made. New, secure entrances and exits were devised to replace those that were known to the enemy and work began on long tunnels offering permanent access to the barracks from several hundred yards away to the northeast and the south. The vital armoured observation posts and gun turrets were repaired, shell proof depots constructed and new positions prepared for machine gunners and riflemen. In addition, the infirmary was enlarged – it suffered from permanent overcrowding – and an extensive internal communication network set up. Life for the garrison was much improved by repairing the southern façade of the barracks with barricades of sandbags so that rough beds could be installed in the barrack rooms, and by providing better facilities for cooking and food

Food storage in a former water cistern. Imperial War Museum Q49840

storage. There were plans for improved lighting and ventilation but it was September before the Germans were able to install more powerful electricity generators and the project for the mechanical ventilation of the fort was never implemented. The generators did, however, enable an electric pump to be run when heavy rain – a constant feature of life at Verdun – flooded the lower galleries of the fort.

Flooding aside, the provision of sufficient water to meet the needs of the garrison remained a great problem. The water cisterns on the lower floor had long since cracked and a plan to supply the fort through underground pipes was never implemented. Every day men had to be sent out on the dangerous task of bringing in the necessary supplies from the ravines to the north of the fort. Casualties were so high on those occasions that water collection fatigues were was known as the *Himmelfahrtskommando* – Ascension parties. The problem eased in August when water was brought to within 300 metres of the fort and it became possible to establish a small reserve.

If, in the words of *Schlachten des Weltkrieges*, Fort Douaumont was soon transformed into an emplacement so 'well-ordered, clean, comfortable and strong' that the troops inside could forget the horrors of the battlefield, the same could not be said of the positions outside. It had become clear during the May offensive that Fort Douaumont would not be able to repel an attack without strong defences in front of it. However, plans to construct a number of strongpoints and to lay a wide field of wire were thwarted by the difficulties of transporting the materials involved and the increased shelling that resulted whenever the work began.

The French plan to retake the fort

On 3 September - one day after Hindenburg suspended German offensive action at Verdun - General Mangin took sole command of all French operations on the Right Bank of the Meuse. Within days, a plan was being prepared for the recapture of both Fort Douaumont and Fort Vaux. Even before the plan was accepted, the work of preparing the terrain had begun. This involved repairing and strengthening the roads needed to bring up supplies, linking the artillery batteries by narrow gauge railway lines and burying telephone cables two metres underground. Facilities at railway stations in the rear were also extended in order to receive the enormous quantities of shells and other supplies – fifteen thousand tons for the artillery and thirty six thousand for the pioneers – needed for the assault. Supply trains arrived at the rate of four or five every day and as soon as night fell, convoys of heavily laden troops and donkeys set off for the front. It was a gigantic task, made worse by weeks of incessant rain. The sector between Souville, Fleury and Thiaumont resembled nothing so much as a vast rubbish dump. The summer's desperate battles had churned the soil to powder, which now turned to sticky mud. For the pioneers, it was a scene of horror. The earth was gorged with corpses. Every blow with pickaxe or shovel struck an obstacle of some sort and the stench was so terrible that the troops put cloves of garlic in their nostrils. There was artillery activity on both sides and while the German response was

The central sector during the late summer of 1916. Service Historique de l'Armée de Terre

limited, it often undid the French preparations as soon as they were completed. It was not just the work that was exhausting; simply reaching the line was a struggle. In daylight the ruins of Fleury or Thiaumont, the railway embankment or the far-off sight of Fort Douaumont could be used for guidance but darkness transformed the area into a featureless wilderness of mud into which men and donkeys slipped and sank.

By now the French possessed air supremacy over the battlefield. The Germans seemed to see two of their own planes for every fifteen French machines. Big biplanes flew over the battlefield controlling and observing fire and, to the great enthusiasm of the French, groups of Nieuport fighters even pursued individual columns of German soldiers on the march.

The task of preparing the front for the coming offensive was pushed on as fast as possible. As the days passed, observation balloons appeared behind French lines. In early October work began on the jump-off trenches. On 9 October General Joffre visited the sector, followed three days later by Georges Clemenceau and other high-ranking visitors, including Field Marshal Sir John French. Clemenceau, who was very keen to visit the front, was sent by Mangin to Fort Souville and returned full of enthusiasm, entertaining Mangin at dinner with comparisons between the French soldiers of the Revolution and those – similar but superior – that he had just met in the line.

By 15 October everything was ready and the French High Command was absolutely confident of success. This time there was to be no mistake. During the weeks preceding the attack Pétain had gathered together over 650 guns of all calibres. German positions along the whole front were to be utterly smashed before the infantry advanced. Artillery preparation was planned down to the smallest detail, with close attention being paid to the prior destruction of wire, shelters and observation posts. To make absolutely sure that there could be no misunderstandings, shortly before the start of the offensive a questionnaire was sent out to seventy four artillery commanders to check that every battery was fully aware of its orders, had sufficient information and that guns and men were ready. For the destruction of Fort Douaumont, the French had two mighty 400mm railway howitzers. These howitzers – with their longer range and greater penetrating power they were more powerful than anything available to the Germans – had been brought up to specially constructed spur lines, where they were kept under camouflage until the weather cleared. With

French 400mm railway howitzer at Baleycourt. The Liberty Memorial Museum, Kansas City, Missouri

typical French humour, the guns were named 'Alsace' and 'Lorraine'.

During September and early October, the French kept up a steady bombardment on the German lines, preventing the troops from repairing their defences or erecting wire. Weeks of rain followed by periods of frost did nothing to improve the situation and the level of desertions started to rise. Exhausted, hungry and isolated, German soldiers stood in mud over their knees on swollen, frostbitten feet with, as their only consolation, the thought that conditions were no better for the French troops opposite. The French, however, did not suffer from constant bombardment and, in addition, their morale was rising as fast as it was sinking for the Germans.

Artillery preparation begins

On 20 October the weather cleared and the French softening-up process began. A roaring avalanche of fire blasted both forward and reserve positions into the air and shattered communications. Gas shells forced troops to wear their masks for hours at a time. The German batteries suffered heavily. They returned fire as well as they could but the shortage of ammunition made it impossible to offer any effective defence and many of their shells fell short, adding to the misery of their own front line. Conditions in the German trenches soon became unbearable. Front line units became cut off from one another, without rations or medical help. It was only by crawling on all fours that messengers could reach the fort.

To trick the Germans into betraying the position of their field guns, General Nivelle ordered a simulated attack for 22 October. In the early afternoon the French guns fell silent and cheers could be heard coming from the French assault trenches. Believing that an attack was imminent, artillery observers urgently called for counter battery fire. In an instant, the German field guns opened up. It was just what

Germans, wearing masks against gas shells, operate a Maxim MG-08.

Nivelle wished. A curtain of fire descended on the German batteries, putting gun after gun out of action until, by 24 October, only ninety were still active out of the one hundred and fifty eight spotted two days earlier.

The volcano of fire raged on for two more days, although the French could have saved their powder; the weather and the fearful bombardment had already broken the defenders' backs. When the prodigious artillery preparation came to an end, almost a quarter of a million shells had been fired. As *Schlachten* remarks, even before the offensive began, French materiel superiority had already won the battle.

Inside Fort Douaumont

Once the French softening-up process began, the German front line troops quickly lost touch with Fort Douaumont. They could see that a line of captive balloons was observing the fort and that French aircraft, keeping watch on the entrances to the fort, were controlling fire with the utmost accuracy, but they had no idea what was happening inside.

In fact, for the defenders inside the fort, it was at first a repeat of the French assault in May and, being well supplied with food, water and ammunition, the garrison of approximately 400 infantry, pioneers and gunners remained optimistic of resisting an attack. There was one factor, however, that might have lessened their optimism. Over the months of non-stop shelling, the protective layer of earth covering Fort Douaumont had been largely blasted away, exposing the concrete to the full force of the shells. Moreover, since 20 October the German occupants of the fort had been able to hear a new sound above the usual noise of the bombardment – the exploding roar of a type of heavy shell unknown until then. From their spur lines near Baleycourt, fourteen kilometres southwest of Fort Douaumont, the two French railway howitzers had gone into action. So far, none of the enormous projectiles had done any serious damage, but it could only be a matter of time before one of them did.

Shortly before midday on 23 October, a gigantic roar drowned the normal thunder of the artillery battle and an abnormally powerful explosion shook Fort Douaumont. A shock wave blasted through the fort, filling the corridors with sulphur fumes. All the lights went out and it was some minutes before the shocked garrison realized what had happened. One of the huge 400mm shells had bored into the earth close to the base of the merlon. A fraction of a second later, its time fuse exploded, blasting into the lower floor where the infirmary was established and instantly killing some fifty wounded and the medical personnel. Shortly afterwards, a second shell came hurtling down. There was a crash and a dull thud, followed almost immediately by the same thunderous roar, and Barrack Room 33 collapsed. As explosion succeeded terrifying explosion, panic began to spread in the fort. With awful regularity the shells continued to fall, bringing down the roof of the main corridor on the ground floor, burying the inmates of several barrack rooms in rubble and blocking access to the northwest machine gun turret, where the observer and telephone officer were killed. Seeing the ground floor corridor blocked, observation impossible, and

Damage to Barrack Room 33 caused by a French 400mm shell. Mémorial de Verdun

several barrack rooms destroyed, most of the garrison took refuge on the lower floor.

It was the sixth shell that delivered the final blow. Slamming through Barrack Room 38, it exploded in the principal pioneer depot on the lower floor, which was filled with machine gun rounds and rockets.[1] There was an earsplitting explosion. The pioneers who were engaged in moving the contents of the depot, disappeared into the flames, as gas and dust filled the corridors. The commandant, Major Rosendahl, was thrown against a wall and knocked unconscious. For a moment it looked as if the terrible explosion of May would be repeated, for next to the pioneer depot – and separated from it by only a single low partition – was a huge store of 7000 hand grenades. Panic began to spread. Crackling flames licked into the corridor and when the wooden staircase which led to the upper floor caught fire, there was a rush for the stone staircase at the other end of the corridor. With Major Rosendahl unable to give orders, the infantry commander, Lieutenant Colonel Schäffer (90th Reserve Infantry), came to a quick decision: Fort Douaumont would be abandoned. It would not be easy to get out – the French had effectively blanketed every exit with gas – but it would be preferable to remaining inside and facing what looked like certain death in a horrendous explosion. Leaving their weapons and equipment behind, the garrison evacuated the fort through the northeastern counterscarp gallery.

In the general confusion, however, the evacuation order did not reach everyone and a group of over 100 men remained behind. Finding the commandant and the fort's long-serving officers gone, *Hauptmann* Soltau (84th Infantry), who had only arrived at the fort a couple of days before and scarcely knew his way around, took command of the fort. He immediately set about clearing the exits and organising the defence of the fort, sending outside all the wounded and gassed who could be evacuated and setting up a machine gun to cover the northwestern entrance.

By nightfall the railway howitzers had ceased their work but heavy shelling continued. Urgent messages by carrier pigeon informing divisional headquarters of the situation and requesting immediate relief were ineffective. Despite courageous attempts to extinguish the fire in the pioneer depot – even using the stock of mineral water kept for the wounded and vats of urine – it continued to burn unabated. By midnight the men were exhausted by their efforts and most were gassed, including Soltau himself and the machine gunners. Runners sent out with messages during the evening – one of them took three hours to cover four kilometres – failed to return. Soltau waited a little longer and when no help came, he ordered the fort to be evacuated.

In the early hours of 24 October, the last of Fort Douaumont's German garrison withdrew. It took two hours to carry out all the wounded. The machine guns were left behind in the hope that relief would arrive during the day. The fort was not quite abandoned, however. The order to leave did not reach two men from the 90th Reserve Infantry who were manning the northwestern counterscarp gallery. Thirty six hours later they were still there.

Shortly after Soltau's group left, the fort's artillery officer, *Hauptmann* Prollius, 108th Field Artillery Regiment, accompanied by

Hauptmann Prollius.
H.P. von Müller's Estate

two officers and a small group of runners from a nearby field battery, returned through the northeastern counterscarp gallery to find Fort Douaumont empty. Making a thorough inspection, Prollius found that it could probably be saved. To his surprise, the gas had dissipated and the fire in the pioneer depot was no longer burning uncontrollably or threatening the magazine alongside it. The upper corridor was smashed in three places but communication from one side of the fort to the other was still possible via the lower floor. Sending out urgent messages to divisional headquarters for machine guns, observers, pioneers, ammunition, food and water, Prollius gathered up any stragglers he could find and soon had a small group with which to defend the fort. The few machine guns that remained operational were set up and the men – some of whom claimed not to be able to handle a machine gun – were ordered to keep the entrances clear at all costs.

Later that morning an exhausted lieutenant from the 27th Reserve Infantry Regiment in the Fleury sector brought the news that the French assault was imminent. In vain Prollius sent out a last message: 'Weak garrison holding fort until reinforcements arrive'. There was no contact with the outside and through the smoke and fumes of the continuing bombardment, nothing at all could be seen.

The French attack

The assault had been fixed for 24 October. From his headquarters at the Moulin de Regret, General Mangin wrote to his wife on 23 October *'Everything is ready. Only rain can stop us...The*

meteorologist has forecast clouds and possible showers but he is
a pessimist. Let us hope. It would be a real pity to have to
postpone the operation'.

The High Command was optimistic. On 23 October Pétain arrived at Verdun, followed the next day by Joffre and a group of English-speaking journalists. Mangin, with fire in his cheeks, looking like 'a wild boar that has scented game', promised Joffre the twenty two front line German battalions within four hours. In typically lively terms he explained his technique:

'I pin down the front line with 75s: nothing can get through
the barrage; then we hammer the trench with 155s and 58s...
When the trench is really turned upside down, we move on. Any
Boche there is ours by then. Generally they come out by units
and surrender.'

The High Command might have been enthusiastic about the operation but the men were not. The name of Verdun was terrifying and the columns that left the town were silent.

By 6 am on 24 October, the assault troops were in position along the whole front. They were laden like mules. In addition to the normal equipment and cartridge pouches 'stuffed to bursting', each man carried two gas masks, three haversacks (one for hardtack, one for meat and chocolate and a third for grenades), two canteens (one for wine and one for water), a blanket rolled in a tent section, an entrenching tool and two empty sandbags. Dawn brought thick fog, but despite the poor visibility General Mangin decided to go ahead with the assault at the arranged time. Intelligence gathered from various sources had shown morale in the German lines to be very low, their positions largely destroyed and the forts seriously damaged. The creeping barrage behind which the infantry was to advance at the rate of 100 metres every four minutes had been carefully planned and did not require observation. The officers, who had been painstakingly instructed in the details of the assault, were provided with compasses. Having taken the decision to continue, the French artillery went into action once again on the German front lines and the rear, swamping the enemy batteries with gas and pouring more heavy shells on Fort Douaumont.

The operation was to take place along a seven kilometre front which, on 24 October, was held by seven German infantry and reserve infantry divisions. It was to be led by the French 38th, 133rd and 74th Divisions which had trained for it intensively at Stainville, near Bar-le-Duc, where a replica of the battlefield – including a full-scale outline

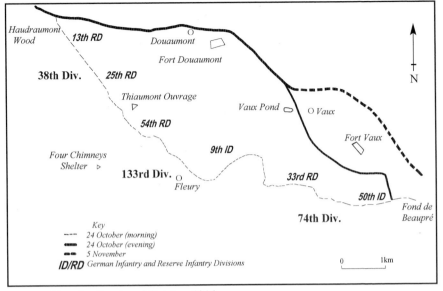

French offensive of October 1916.

of Fort Douaumont – had been laid out. Stretching from Haudraumont Wood, on the western side of Fort Douaumont, to the Fond de Beaupré below Fort Vaux, the front was divided into three sectors. On the right, General Lardemelle's 74th Division was to retake Fort Vaux. In the centre, General Passaga's 133rd Division, nicknamed '*La Gauloise*', was to retake the heights above Fleury before moving on to the German strongholds of Caillette Wood, Fausse-Côte Ravine and the machine gun turret to the east of the fort. On the left, the important sector that included Douaumont village and Fort Douaumont fell to the 38th Division under General Guyot de Salins. The 38th Division was largely made up of African troops, among them Senegalese and Somalis, profoundly dreaded by the Germans because of their ruthless way with captives.

Opposite the 38th, German lines were held by the 13th and 25th Reserve Divisions and – covering Fort Douaumont in the vital sector between the Thiaumont *ouvrage* and Fleury – the 54th Division.

The honour of taking Fort Douaumont itself had fallen to three battalions of the distinguished *Régiment d'Infanterie Coloniale du Maroc* (RICM) commanded by Lieutenant Colonel Régnier. The RICM was an elite regiment which, despite its name, was an exclusively French formation raised originally from troops on service in Morocco, to which Senegalese or Somali units might be attached in exceptional circumstances. They were to jump off along a 500 metre front which ran from a position just below the Thiaumont *ouvrage*

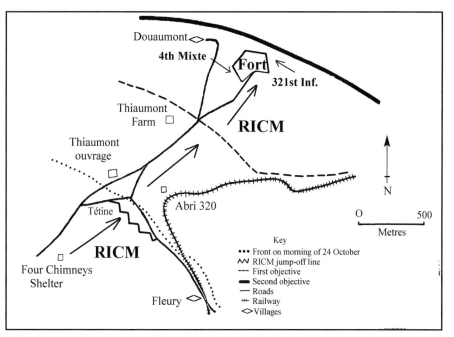

The recapture of Fort Douaumont on 24 October 1916.

known as the *'Tétine'* to a point approximately half way along the road
to Fleury. The three RICM battalions (4th, 1st and 8th) were drawn up
in succession with the 4th in the lead. The leading battalion was to
seize the enemy's front lines and dig in half way to the fort. Leaving
the 4th in position, the 1st Battalion was then to move forward, encircle
the fort and take up positions to the north of it. The 8th Battalion,
supported by flame thrower units, would seize the fort and hold it.

Jump-off was fixed for 11.40am. The RICM had a difficult time at
the beginning. The slippery and waterlogged terrain slowed them down
and, to make matters worse, a German unit had penetrated into the 4th
Battalion's forward positions during the night – the trenches had been
evacuated overnight to avoid the coming artillery preparation – and set
up a machine gun. The hail of bullets flying unexpectedly from a
position believed to be French caused a moment of confusion but the
machine gun was quickly overcome and the 4th continued across the
chaotic terrain, throwing away their heavy packs and haversacks as
they went. Pressing on with difficulty – for one member of the 4th
Battalion the battlefield was so destroyed that he could not imagine
how it had looked before – they overcame pockets of bitter resistance
to reach German dug-outs along a destroyed railway line, where they
took scores of prisoners, some of whom claimed to have had no food
for six days.

Jump-off trench in the Douaumont sector. Service Historique de l'Armée de Terre

The operation went well along the front as a whole. Having reached their first objective, all three divisions moved off again at 1.40pm with units leap-frogging over each other as each goal was attained. On the right 74th Division was held up, but in the centre resistance was quickly overcome and troops from 133rd Division ploughed on towards the fort and the machine gun turret on the ridge to the east. On the left, units from 38th Division quickly seized Couleuvre Ravine and

French troops attacking in October 1916. Service Historique de l'Armée de Terre

took the crest of the ridge above it but were prevented from advancing into Helly Ravine by their own artillery fire. Moving quickly, elements of the 4th *Régiment Mixte de Zouaves et Tirailleurs* seized Douaumont village at 2.45 pm. While forward units dug in some sixty metres to the north of the village, others penetrated as far as the western ditch of Fort Douaumont and linked up with the RICM.

The 4th Battalion of the RICM had reached the first objective at 1pm. At 1.40 pm the French artillery ceased shelling Fort Douaumont and, leaving the 4th to consolidate the position, the 1st Battalion moved on towards the fort believing the 8th to be close behind. The going was very difficult. Hammered for days by the French artillery, the battlefield looked as if a cyclone had passed over it. As far as the eye could see there was nothing but shell holes and lakes of mud, from which emerged horribly mutilated corpses, many of which had lain there since May. When, a short distance from the fort, the fog suddenly cleared, the 1st Battalion realized that the 8th was nowhere to be seen. Not wishing to give the Germans time to react, the commander of the leading company of the 1st Battalion, Captain Dorey, ordered the battalion forward onto the fort. Electrified by the sight of the stronghold before them, a torrent of men surged into the ditches led, out of breath but full of energy, by the stout captain himself. On the superstructure, they met elements of the 321st Infantry who, having already reached their objectives on the right of the fort without seeing any sign of the RICM, had crossed the eastern ditch and seized the northeastern machine gun turret and observation post.

The 8th Battalion came up a few minutes later, having been delayed by a compass error. From the regimental command post in Four Chimneys Shelter the 800 men of the 8th Battalion, reinforced by a company of pioneers, had set off for the front lines at 11am, where they arrived just after jump-off. By then the German counter barrage had begun and they began to suffer heavily. Expecting to link up with the

1st Battalion, *Commandant* Nicolay – a tall man with handsome *gauloises* moustaches who reminded his men of a cavalry officer from an earlier age – led them on through the fog, guided by the compass. After some time, with the landscape looking different than expected, Nicolay began to wonder if they were off course. A patrol picked up a German soldier – a former waiter in a Paris café – who pointed out the direction of the fort and Nicolay realised that the compass needle had been deflected by iron and steel debris on the battlefield.

Nicolay now ordered the men to change direction and, tired as they were from the effort of crossing the battlefield, a wave of euphoria set in among them. Meeting little resistance, they reached Fort Douaumont at approximately 3pm and relieved the 1st Battalion, which moved on to its original objectives two hundred metres to the north. Using automatic rifles, grenades and flame throwers, colonials and pioneers immediately set to work to clear the fort. The German defenders fought valiantly but faced with such overwhelming numbers, prolonged resistance was hopeless.

Inside Fort Douaumont, the fire in the pioneer depot had begun to burn again. Calling his officers together, *Hauptmann* Prollius asked each one for his opinion. All agreed that they had no choice but to surrender. In silence, maps and papers were destroyed and the garrison of four officers and twenty four men gathered in one of the barrack rooms. When the first French soldiers penetrated the lower floor of the barracks, a lieutenant went towards them with hands raised.

The German occupation of Fort Douaumont was over. It had been captured – and recaptured – virtually empty. It was a strange fate for a fort which, as General Rouquerol wrote, 'was for eight months the key to a battlefield soaked with the blood of hundreds of thousands of men and hammered by millions upon millions of shells'.

Outside the fort, units of the 4th Battalion now re-established direct liaison with Verdun while the remainder joined the 1st Battalion in covering the fort and providing external security. Inside, the 8th carried out a thorough inspection of the premises. Guards were posted in the underground access tunnels, telephones lines were cut and magazines and stores opened. Filthy and damaged as it was, Fort Douaumont, with its electric lights, comfortable beds, telephones, radio and 'Kasino', seemed to the French troops a haven of peace and comfort. Prollius, who spoke French, offered his quarters to the new French commander but the offer was proudly refused by Nicolay, who preferred to sleep the first night at the entrance to the fort with his men. Having offered to put out the fire in the pioneer depot, Prollius gathered up his small group of men, put on breathing equipment and set to work.

Thus Fort Douaumont passed back into French hands after eight months of German occupation. Mangin was delighted, writing to his wife that the whole operation passed off 'like a ballet'. Once the troops had disappeared into the fog, hours passed before any news came back. General Passaga, 'devoured by misgivings and tortured by anxiety' while waiting for news at his command post in Fort Souville, found the effort of remaining calm and demonstrating confidence to be the worst test of leadership. At 2.45 pm a sudden ray of sunshine split the fog and, to the delight of the observers peering through binoculars into the murk, French soldiers could be seen silhouetted on top of the fort. A little over an hour later, a plane from 133rd Division dropped a fragment of a map showing the French line level with and a little to the right of Fort Douaumont. Along the front as a whole, almost all the objectives of the day had been achieved and many guns and prisoners taken. French losses, however, had been severe. The four days of the counteroffensive had resulted in 47,000 casualties. In the attack on Fort Douaumont alone the RICM had lost twenty three officers and 829 men. *Commandant* Nicolay's battalion

The Bussiere gun turret at Fort Souville used by General Mangin during the October assault on Fort Douaumont. The Liberty Memorial Museum, Kansas City, Missouri

returned with few more than 100 of the 800 men who had arrived at Verdun on 20 October.

Nevertheless, it was a great French victory and the French public received it with joy. Donations to the French war loan rose dramatically – on hearing the news one woman immediately donated 300,000 gold francs – while Mangin received the insignia of a Grand Officer of the *Légion d'Honneur* and had his portrait painted. In a special ceremony organised at Stainville – where the victorious colonials were allowed an entire week to celebrate their victory – the President of France decorated the regimental colours with the Cross of the *Légion d'Honneur*, the first time that any French regiment had been awarded so high a decoration for an achievement other than capturing the colours of the enemy. To the great satisfaction of his men, Nicolay was also awarded the *Légion d'Honneur* and promoted to lieutenant colonel.

In the German camp, however, the news was received with deep emotion. Soon after the operation General Nivelle was told by the Duke of Connaught that, on receiving news of the capture of Fort Douaumont, his cousin, the Crown Prince of Germany, 'cried much and swore much and finally took a great oath to take back everything that [the French] had taken from him'. To soften the blow, the German public was informed that Fort Douaumont was to have been evacuated in favour of a better position but nothing could hide the reality of the situation. The cornerstone of French defence at Verdun, the finest observation point in the area from which the movement of no German unit was hidden, was finally back in French hands.

Final counteroffensive

On the morning of 25 October the French front lines ran a short distance to the north of Fort Douaumont. The position was not entirely safe, however, since the Germans still controlled important observatories at Fort Vaux, Hardaumont and Pepper Hill from which they could direct fire on the fort and the surrounding sectors. Accordingly, within a day or two of the fort's recapture, a fresh French offensive was launched, as a result of which Fort Vaux was retaken on 2 November.

This success was followed on 15 December by a further major offensive along an eleven kilometre front, during which the newly repaired 155mm turret on Fort Douaumont went into action for the first time in support of the French infantry. Preparations for the offensive involved the laying of thirty kilometres of roads and ten

Four Chimneys Shelter. The 8th Battalion of the RICM moved off from here on 24 October 1916.. Service Historique de l'Armée de Terre

kilometres of narrow gauge railway lines, in addition to the construction of trenches, depots and magazines. At 10am on 15 December, four French divisions jumped off in bitterly cold weather.

The state of the fort after recapture. Mémorial de Verdun

The operation was successful in recapturing the destroyed villages of Vacherauville and Louvemont (both of which had been in German hands since the previous February), as well as Hardaumont and Pepper Hill. With the front now three kilometres to the north and all the important observatories once more in French hands, Fort Douaumont was finally safe.

1. There is some dispute over the precise point of entry and the calibre of the shell that caused the fire in the pioneer depot. A plan of Fort Douaumont drawn up after the battle, which is now to be found in the Bibiothèque Municipale at Verdun, shows the impact of each 400mm and 420mm shell on the fort. No impact is shown over Barrack Room 38 and it is clear from the state of the masonry that the roof of the barrack room has not been replaced. It is possible that rather than hitting the top of the barrack block the shell flew in through the destroyed facade and slammed into the pioneer depot through the gaping hole in the floor of Barrack Room 38 left by the explosion of 8 May. As the explosion of a 400mm shell would have left visible evidence on the lower floor, some historians argue that the shell that caused the fire must have been of a lighter calibre. Being unable to resolve the question, the author has followed the version in *Schlachten des Weltkrieges*.

Chapter Six

AFTER THE BATTLE

Fort Douaumont may have been safe, but it was in a terrible state. During the four days of the October offensive the fort had been hammered by thousands of shells, almost a hundred of which came from the two giant railway guns at Baleycourt. Gaping holes had been torn in the roof. The underground tunnels and the principal ground floor corridor were blocked with debris and several inches deep in mud and water. The southern facade of the fort had been shot away, as had the barbed wire entanglements on the glacis and the iron railing along the bottom of the ditch. The counterscarp was largely demolished and, on the south side, the ditch had completely disappeared. The top of the fort was covered with massive shell holes and the whole area was littered with shreds of clothing, smashed weapons, bleached bones and rusting equipment.

In the weeks immediately following the recapture of Fort Douaumont and despite a ceaseless bombardment, the new garrison set about consolidating the position. Hygiene was a very serious problem. While largely habitable, many of the barrack rooms were filled with dirt and debris from the tunneling work, and others had been used as

Shell-damaged southern facade. Note the light railway line in the centre of the picture. The Liberty Memorial Museum, Kansas City, Missouri

The top of Fort Douaumont in December 1916. Mémorial de Verdun

mortuaries or sanitary facilities. These now had to be entirely cleaned and disinfected. The accompanying infestation of rats (whose numbers were too great for the little grey cat that the French found in the fort and nicknamed 'Prollia') was systematically poisoned. Water remained a problem – while plenty of water seeped into the barracks from the top of the fort, it was polluted and had to be filtered and chlorinated. The situation only improved when wells were dug and reserve water tanks installed. As the months went by, showers, laundry and sanitary facilities were installed, as well as lighting, heating and electrically driven air pumps. Attempts to combat the infiltration of gas during shelling by filters fitted behind the air vents were, however, only partially successful, since gas also seeped in through cracks and fissures in the superstructure. Early in 1918 a branch of the American YMCA was opened in one of the barrack rooms. White-painted corrugated iron covered the roof and the walls were decorated with flags. Tables and chairs, books and a phonograph completed the installation, which was inaugurated on 16 February.

A view of the 155mm turret and the NE machnine gun turret in 1919.

NORTHEASTERN MACHINE GUN TURRET   155mm GUN TURRET

To improve and strengthen the fort's battered defences the southern side of the barracks was rebuilt, and protected by the installation of machine guns. The counterscarp galleries and Bourges Casemate were repaired and wire erected in the ditches and on the glacis. Inspection of the armoured turrets showed that they had resisted the months of shelling surprisingly well. The 75mm turret could only turn through a quarter of its circumference and needed some repair but, to the surprise of the new French artillery officer, the 155mm turret had only to be thoroughly cleaned and greased before it was operational again. The machine gun turrets, which had never been intended to resist heavy-calibre shelling, were, however, seriously damaged. Following repair of the rotation and eclipse mechanisms, two machine guns were installed in the northeastern turret, but the damaged northwestern turret was replaced by an observation post. Modern telephone and radio facilities provided for communication within the fort and to the rear as far as Bar-le-Duc.

In February 1917, command of Fort Douaumont passed to Captain Harispe, a resourceful man who had commanded Fort Moulainville during the Battle of Verdun. Following his appointment a plan was drawn up to excavate deep, well-ventilated tunnels under the fort that would not only connect all the defensive elements with the central barrack block but, at the same time, protect the garrison from the psychological strain of prolonged bombardment. In the centre of the fort a thirty-metre deep pit was dug, from which tunnels were excavated to the gun turrets, Bourges Casemate and counterscarp galleries. The aim of this work was to transform the barracks and the gun turrets into independent combat positions, capable of prolonged resistance. Further information about the tunnel system is to be found in Tour No 3.

Supplying the fort was very difficult, as the months of shelling and heavy rain had left the ground – in the words of one French writer – as soft as mayonnaise. To improve the situation, duckboards were laid on

The same view in 2001.

NORTHEASTERN MACHINE GUN TURRET   155mm GUN TURRET

Approach track to Fort Douaumont after the battle.

trestles from the nearest road and narrow gauge railways constructed, one of which ultimately ran into the barrack block. A strong communication trench, the *Boyau de Londres*, linked the fort to the rear and shell proof access to the barracks at all times was provided by the new long tunnels to Caillette Ravine and the hillside south of the fort. However, the supply problem was not completely solved. Ration parties could only be sent out from the fort during lulls in shelling and ropes were always carried to pull back onto the duckboards anyone who slipped off into the mud.

Thus repaired and garrisoned, Fort Douaumont continued to play an active role in the defence of Verdun up to the end of the war. It received many visitors, including, in January 1918, the fort's *marraine de guerre* – or patron – Madame Benoist d'Azy, who arrived in the company of an American delegation. Having toured the fort, where several bottles of champagne were drunk, the visitors prepared to return only to find – to the commandant's horror – that *la marraine* had disappeared. A frantic search was carried out to no avail and, as it was getting late and the regular German shelling was about to begin, the other visitors departed. As soon as they had left Madame Benoist d'Azy reappeared. Not wishing to leave the fort so early she had hidden herself in a room adjoining the commandant's quarters, having arranged with the orderly to stand guard outside the door. The garrison was delighted, the cook surpassed himself with a stew of *singe* – tinned beef, which the men called 'monkey meat' – and, wrapped up in the commandant's cloak and wearing a helmet, Mme. Benoist d'Azy finally left the fort at 2am.

German troops on Fort Douaumont again in 1940.
H.P. von Müller's Estate

After the Armistice, Fort Douaumont was left in its wartime state and partially opened for visits. During the 1930s – when Cordt von Brandis was once again a visitor – steps were taken to strengthen certain defensive elements, including the deep tunnels and some of the armoured turrets. Despite that, in June 1940, Fort Douaumont fell again to the Germans after brief combat. To many German soldiers – including, no doubt, to Eugen Radtke who returned in 1941 to attend ceremonies commemorating the twenty-fifth anniversary of the battle – it must have seemed as if the battle for Fort Douaumont had finally been won.

Generalmajor **Haupt explaining to German troops in August 1940 how he stormed the fort in 1916.** Bundersarchive Koblenz. Bild 183/L25203

Epilogue

The Battle of Verdun was characterized by an intense ten-month bombardment that turned the battlefield into a sea of mud. Trenches, shelters, batteries and communications were annihilated, yet Fort Douaumont survived. After the war was over, it was calculated that the fort had been battered by a minimum of 120,000 shells, of which at least 2000 were of a calibre greater than 270mm. Only the French 400mm and German 420mm shells succeeding in piercing the concrete carapace. Even though the stone-built façade of the barracks was demolished, the lower floor remained habitable throughout the battle. After the war, French military engineers studied the strengths and weaknesses of Fort Douaumont and used their findings in the design of a new chain of concrete-covered underground forts that was specifically designed to prevent the Germans from ever again invading France from the east. This was the Maginot Line.

Not all those who had been involved in the battles of 1916 lived to see the construction of the Maginot Line. *Hauptmann* Kalau von Hofe – the only commandant of the fort to be decorated with the *Pour le Mérite* for his part in retaining it in German hands – was killed on the Chemin des Dames in April 1917. Sergeant Wiedenhus disappeared in Caillette Wood on 13 May 1916. *Hauptmann* Soltau was killed in a tank battle at Cambrai in 1917. *Commandant* Nicolay died of wounds received at Louvemont in the French offensive of December 1916 and General Mangin died suddenly in Paris in 1925 amid unconfirmed rumours that he was poisoned. Of those who did witness its construction, General Pétain was fated to arrange an armistice with the Germans in June 1940. *Hauptmann* Prollius was killed in a bombing raid over Hanover in 1942 and Haupt died in Berlin in 1944, having risen to the rank of *Generalmajor*. Brandis and Radtke both lived to see the fiftieth anniversary of the Battle of Verdun, but only Brandis was invited to meet General de Gaulle at the official ceremonies in Paris. To the end of his life, Radtke never received general recognition for his part in the capture of Fort Douaumont.

In August 1914, André Maginot, after whom the new fortress line was named, was a Member of Parliament for Bar-le-Duc. Immediately volunteering for service – despite parliamentary immunity – Maginot took the train to Verdun to join his regiment, the 44th Territorial Infantry, part of which formed the garrison of Fort Douaumont. A few days later the newly mobilized Territorials made camp in a clearing close to the country road from Douaumont village to Bezonvaux, little

The Maginot Monument close to Fort Souville.

dreaming that in February 1916 the same road would be crossed by Radtke, Haupt and Brandis on their way to the fort. The Territorials were a cheerful group and Maginot's memoir of patrols and ambushes among the villages below the fort is high-spirited and carefree.

Between Maginot and his comrades, going blithely to war in the blue jackets and red trousers of the French army of 1914, and the filthy and exhausted men on both sides who fought so tenaciously for Fort Douaumont throughout 1916 there are two years of a type of warfare that few could have imagined. From its horrors there was no escape. For those men the best epitaph comes in the words of a German author of a later generation: *Wieder einmal haben Männer Geschichte gemacht.*

Once again, men have made history

Chapter Seven

A CAR TOUR AND THREE WALKS
WITHIN THIS AREA

This section describes three battlefield walks that have been chosen to illustrate the events described in this book. It also includes a car tour of the general area that includes some of the lesser known rear sites mentioned in the text.

For visitors wishing to walk other sectors further suggestions are available in *Walking Verdun: A Guide to the Battlefield* in the Battleground Europe series.

Tour No. 1 – The Douaumont fortified sector

Duration – Three Hours
Length – Approximately eight kilometres
*Douaumont Ossuary - Douaumont village – Fort Douaumont –
Machine gun turret to the east of the fort – Combat Shelter DV1 –
Abri 320 – Douaumont Ossuary.*

This walking/cycling tour is covered by both IGN Blue Series Map No. 3212 *Ouest* and by the special IGN map No. 3112 ET, entitled *Forêts de Verdun et du Mort-Homme - Champ de Bataille de Verdun*. It does not cover Fort Douaumont itself, which is described in Tours 2 and 3. It is not a difficult walk, although the forest paths are likely to remain muddy all year. The suggested time allows for a leisurely inspection of the sites visited. To accompany the walk, a plan is provided below. **Please note that this route cannot be walked on Mondays and Tuesdays, when the firing range is in operation.**

The tour begins at the Douaumont Ossuary **(1)**. The Ossuary stands on a bare hillside at the head of Dame Ravine (on modern maps this ravine is marked as the *Ravin de la Mort*). At the beginning of 1916, this hillside was the site of a number of concrete batteries and infantry entrenchments which, together with a combat shelter, have entirely disappeared. A number of memorials are to be seen on the western side of the Ossuary. These include the large memorial to Jewish soldiers of

France, the allied nations and foreign volunteers, who died for France during the First World War. Its design recalls the Western Wall of the Temple and the two tablets are inscribed with the beginning of each of the Ten Commandments.

The Ossuary was inaugurated on 7 August 1932 and owes its origin to the work of Monsignor Ginisty, Archbishop of Verdun from 1914 to 1946, who travelled the world to raise money to build a final resting place for the men whose bones scattered the battlefield. The building is said to represent the hilt of a sword that has been thrust into the ground against the invader.

Inside the Ossuary, the central gallery is 137 metres long and houses forty six stone 'coffins' set in alcoves. Each alcove commemorates a particular sector of the battlefield and any human remains found in that sector are placed in the corresponding vault on the lower floor. The Douaumont alcove is immediately on the right of the chapel by the entrance to the tower. At the top of the tower, orientation tables in the window ledges help to identify the principal features of the battlefield. Although Fort Douaumont is only just visible from the tower, the extensive panorama brings out clearly

The Ossuary and the monument to Muslim soldiers in 2001.

Plan to accompany Tour No. 1: the Douaumont fortified sector.

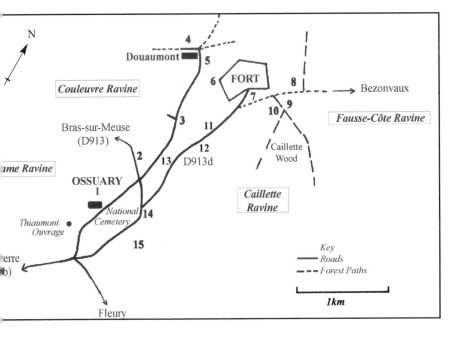

the strategic importance of the Douaumont-Froideterre Ridge.

The chapel has an interesting series of memorial windows. The first window on the right and the last window on the left commerate to Lieutenant François Guéneau de Mussy, the commander of 8 Company, 129th Infantry, who was killed on Fort Douaumont on 22 May 1916. The last window before the altar on the right hand side is an unusual memorial to nurses who served in the Verdun Sector in 1917. Mass is said in the chapel at 10am on the first Sunday of each month. The national cemetery in front of the Ossuary contains the graves of 15,000 French soldiers, a section on the left hand side being dedicated to Muslim soldiers in French regiments. Close to the Muslim section stands the Islamic memorial, which looks like a small mosque. This new addition to the monuments commemorates all Muslim soldiers who died for France during the First World War. It was inaugurated by President Chirac of France in June 2006.

On leaving the Ossuary, stand with your back to the main door, then turn left and walk or cycle along the road at the top of the cemetery until you reach the nearby junction with the D913. Do not take the road on your left, which leads to Bras-sur-Meuse, passing the *Abri des Pélérins* cafè **(2)** and restaurant. The buildings opposite the cafe stand close to the site of Thiaumont Farm. Take the road opposite you, which leads to the destroyed village of Douaumont. The warning sign on the left of the road that refers to the use of the firing range on Mondays and Tuesdays does not prevent travellers from visiting the village, or from taking the footpath between the village and the fort. Continue towards the village until you come to a small wire enclosure and high wooden gate **(3)** on the left hand side of the road, behind which is a radio mast. Although the forest is too thick to see it, you are now at the top of the ridge between Couleuvre Ravine (on your right) and Dame Ravine (on your left). Stand facing the wooden gate. At this point, Morchée Trench would have been directly in front of you, with the Bonnet-d'Evêque position a little way along the road on your right. Fontaine Trench ran along the right hand side of this road, approximately 200 metres beyond Bonnet-d'Evêque.

Continue along the road towards Douaumont village **(4)**. This village, one of the nine villages on the battlefield to be entirely destroyed during 1916, has never been rebuilt. A signboard provides information about the villages in four languages, and short posts set in the ground indicate the site of each house, as well as giving the name and type of work carried out by the inhabitants. A plan of the village and fort is to be seen at the junction of the two streets. The new chapel

The new chapel on the site of Douaumont church. Machine guns in the spire of the church caused many casualties among the Germans approaching Fort Douaumont from the north on 25 February 1916.

stands on the site of the original church, from whose tower deadly French machine guns swept the glacis and the top of Fort Douaumont, causing many casualties among the German attackers on 25 February. Paintings on the chapel walls illustrate peaceful rural life in Douaumont before the First World War.

As you face the gate into the chapel, the high trees to your right mark the edge of Helly Ravine, which was the site of an important German encampment. The ravine was retaken from the Germans by the 4th *Régiment Mixte de Zouaves et Tirailleurs* on 24 October 1916, at which time it was entirely devoid of trees.

Return towards the junction of the two village streets and face the chapel. The track on your left is the pre-war country road that ran from Douaumont village to Bras-sur-Meuse, where it joined the main road to Verdun. It follows the high ridge between Helly Ravine and Couleuvre Ravine that formed an important observatory during the battle.

Return to the parking area and stand with your back to the village. The road on your left is the old country road from Douaumont to Bezonvaux, which was crossed by the Brandenburgers as they approached Fort Douaumont on 25 February 1916. It leads onto a modern firing range and is inaccessible, as is the track immediately opposite.

Now take the path to be seen at the edge of the trees on the other side of the road **(5)**. It is signposted *Fort de Douaumont 800 metres*. When you enter the forest, you are on the glacis of Fort Douaumont and here the signs of shelling are extremely impressive. The path leads uphill towards the northwestern angle of the ditch **(6)**, from where the northwestern machine gun turret is visible at the top of the earth rampart. The northwestern counterscarp gallery is to be seen in the corner of the ditch below. Even though the ditch is shallower today than in 1916 and the counterscarp railing is missing, this approach gives an indication of the original strength of Fort Douaumont. The dangers of approaching it over the open glacis in 1916 can easily be imagined.

The path continues along the top of the counterscarp to the car park **(7)**. Cross the car park to the notice board at the back of the car parking area and follow the signpost to the *Batterie et Tourelle Est de Douaumont, Monument du 74 RI*. Like the glacis, this area has been heavily shelled and the effect is even more remarkable during the winter, when the shell holes are full of water.

The memorial to the 3rd Battalion of the 74th Infantry Regiment is approximately 400 metres from Fort Douaumont **(8)**. It stands on the site of a retractable gun turret and observation post that was unfinished when war broke out. Adjacent to the turret was a concrete battery. By August 1914 the entrance to the turret, the rooms on the lower floor and the shaft of the observation post had been completed, but the twin short barrelled 75mm guns and the armoured cupolas were not yet in place. In 1915, the gun turret was transformed into a shelter by the addition of a thick cover of concrete, while the observation turret became a machine gun position covering the interval between this ridge and Fort Vaux.

The Germans captured this position - known as Panzerturm 637 or, more usually, Panzerturm Ost - on 26 February 1916. It very quickly became extremely important, since it dominated Caillette Ravine, through which the French could reinforce the front line. As an observation post, this position provided secure facilities for directing artillery fire over French positions in Caillette Wood and it also served as a command post and dressing station.

On 22 May 1916 the 3rd Battalion of the French 74th Infantry under Commandant Lefèbvre-Dibon attacked this position as part of the first attempt to retake Fort Douaumont. Under heavy fire the French fought their way to this ridge taking, as they did so, combat shelter *(Abri de Combat)* DV1 and a former ammunition depot at the edge of Caillette Wood. Having taken the machine gun turret after bloody hand-to-hand fighting, the 74th realized that it was alone, since the units on the left and right had been unable to advance. Messengers, sent out to re-establish liaison with headquarters, were captured. Seeing himself alone and under threat of attack from three sides, Lefèbvre-Dibon set up his command post in the former ammunition depot and held out

Panzerturm 637. H.P. von Müller's Estate

until the afternoon of 23 May, when he was forced to surrender. In twenty five hours his battalion had lost 72.2% of its effectives.

The heavy forest cover makes it impossible today to understand the importance of the ridge on which this memorial stands. There is no trace of the entrance to the turret and the lower floor is inaccessible. The adjacent battery has completely disappeared.

Continue along the path away from the fort and turn right at the end. If you are using IGN map 3112 ET, the forest block opposite you here is 354. After approximately 200 metres, turn right again on the *Sentier de Douaumont* (on the IGN maps this track is marked *Chemin de la Plume*). The forest block opposite is now 359. Continue for approximately 500 metres and turn left downhill at the signpost that reads *Abris d'Infanterie DV1, DV2, Etang de Vaux*. Combat shelter DV1 (Douaumont-Vaux 1) is approximately 250 metres downhill **(9)**.

This combat shelter, which was known to the Germans as *I-Werk Nord*, was constructed in 1907 to accommodate infantry serving in the retrenchments in the Douaumont sector. DV1 housed a half company in two rooms measuring four metres by ten metres. There was a kitchen in a third room and a latrine at the end of the shelter. The concrete walls were two metres thick and the reinforced concrete roof was one metre thick. A protective stone wall in front of the shelter provided cover for the entrance. The lower floor contained a water cistern and the whole area was surrounded by barbed wire.

DV1 is a total ruin. The protective wall has been completely destroyed, leaving the two rooms open to view. There is no trace of the barbed wire that surrounded the shelter and no access to the cisterns on

DV1, scene of fourteen desperate German attacks. The protective wall was completely destroyed, leaving the rooms open to view.

the lower floor. Between 27 February and 2 April the shelter was the scene of no less than fourteen desperate German attacks, which included the use of flame throwers and even an attempt at mining. DV1 was finally captured by the 120th Württemburg Reserve Infantry Regiment on 2 April 1916. It was recaptured by the French on 22 May but retaken the next day by units of the German 20th and 24th Infantry Regiments. The shelter finally returned to French hands on 24 October. Visitors who wish to get an idea of the original design of a combat shelter should visit the signposted shelters PC 119 or FT 1 on the ridge between the ruined Thiaumont *ouvrage* and the *Ouvrage de Froideterre.*

Opposite DV1 on the left front is Caillette Wood. The site of the ammunition depot **(10)** in which Lefèbvre-Dibon made his headquarters is to the right front, close to the corner formed by the meeting of the two tracks in front of the shelter. One of twenty nine in the Verdun sector, the depot, known as *dépôt intermédiare 'g'*, was constructed in 1889 to supply the batteries in the sector if the sector magazine was unable to do so. Constructed in a steep hillside and served by a narrow gauge railway, the depot formed a long chamber, three and a half metres wide and almost seventeen and a half metres long. Today there is no trace of the depot apart from a long excavation into the hillside and the occasional short section of railway line. Visitors wishing to obtain an idea of the original appearance should visit the *Dépôt de munitions* below the *Ouvrage de Froideterre.*

After visiting DVI, retrace your steps uphill to the *Sentier de Douaumont (Chemin de la Plume)* and turn left. This will take you back towards the fort. On reaching the road, turn left towards the Ossuary.

The *Boyau de Londres.*

The recently restored graves of two unknown French soldiers are to be seen on the left a short distance beyond the car park. A little further on, a footpath to the right signposted *Stèles Basques 40 mètres* leads through an area of deep shell holes to the graves of three casualties of the unsuccessful French attempt to retake Fort Douaumont in May 1916. As you continue towards the Ossuary you will pass several interesting features including, on the right, the ruins of infantry shelters TD3 *(Abri 2408)* **(11)** and TD2 *(Abri Adalbert)* **(13)**, which are almost as damaged as the Thiaumont fieldwork. In 1916, batteries flanked the combat shelters but no trace of them can to be seen today and the ground inside the wood is a mass of shell holes. A French plan to link *Abri 2408* with the Bourges Casemate at Fort Douaumont, drawn up in 1917, was never implemented. On the left hand side of the road, between the shelters, is a well excavated section of the *Boyau de Londres* **(12)**, a strong communication trench that connected Belleville Ridge to Fort Douaumont via Froideterre and *Abri 320*. The present appearance of the trench dates from refurbishment carried out in 1917. A short distance beyond the *Boyau de Londres*, a sign on the left

Combat Shelter TD3, close to Fort Douaumont.

Heavy shelling on *Abri 320*. Caillette Ravine is behind the trees on the left.

reading *61ième RAD 400 mètres* points to a memorial to five members of a field artillery regiment who were killed by shelling in July 1917 while digging shelters in an adjacent ravine.

Continue towards the Ossuary. At the junction with the D913, turn left by the monument **(14)** to the *Soldat du Droit*, André Thomé, a member of the French parliament who was killed on 10 March 1916, aged 36. Continue along the D913 with the Ossuary on your right until you reach a path on the left that leads to *Abri 320* **(15)**. This brick-lined shelter, ten metres below ground level, measured three and a half metres by seventy metres and provided accommodation for reserves. Two small rooms at each entrance served as command posts and ventilation was provided by two 'chimneys'. Originally, two steep flights of steps led down into the shelter but only one entrance is visible today. This shelter, which was captured from the French 39th Infantry Regiment on 23 June 1916, was known to the Germans as M-*Raum 372* (ammunition depot). During the operation to retake Fort Douaumont in October 1916 *M-Raum 372* was used as a battalion and sector command post and, in addition, was filled with reserves, wounded, stretcher bearers and messengers. After Fort Douaumont was recaptured on 24 October 1916, the occupants of the *M-Raum* found themselves encircled and, fearing the explosion of a depot of hand grenades inside the shelter, they surrendered.

After visiting *Abri 320*, return to the Ossuary where the tour ends.

TOUR NO. 2
A tour of the ditch and superstructure
Duration – Two hours

For this tour, visitors may find it helpful to use the accompanying numbered plan below.

Visitors should note that the reconstruction work that began in 2001 is intended to restore the 1917 appearance to Fort Douaumont. As a result, certain features of the facade mentioned in this tour may disappear.

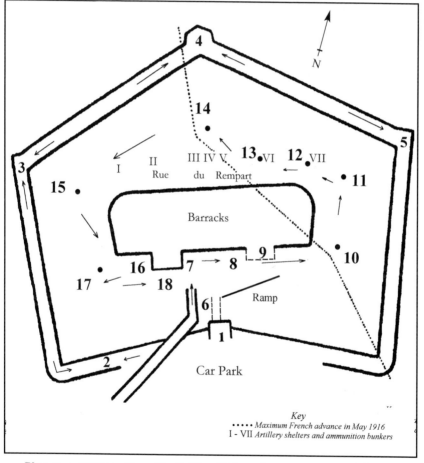

Plan to accompany Tour No. 2. The ditch and superstructure of Fort Douaumont.

NORTHWESTERN COUNTERSCARP GALLERY

NORTHWESTERN MACHINE GUN TURRET

WESTERN ENTRANCE TO BARRACKS

MERLON

BOURGES CASEMATE

RUINED ENTRANCE BLOCKHOUSE

Aerial view of the fort's defensive features. Jean-Luc Kaluzko

The main entrance – 1

The tour begins in the car park of Fort Douaumont.

The car park occupies part of the site of the glacis and ditch on the south side of the fort. If you had stood in this area before February 1916, you would have been outside the ditch. To your left, the wagon road from the direction of the Thiaumont *ouvrage*, roughly following the line of the present road, ran up a long slope to the guard house that stood at the top of the outer wall of the ditch. It then ran down into the ditch and entered the tunnel to be seen to your right front. Passing under the inner wall of the ditch, this tunnel came to an end outside the lower floor of the barracks, where two ramps rising to ground floor level provided access to the eastern and western ends of the barrack

75MM GUN TURRET

NORTHERN COUNTERSCARP GALLERY

1917 OBSERVATION POST

OBSERVATION POST

NORTH EASTERN MACHINE GUN TURRET

BARRACKS

SOUTHERN ENTRANCE TO BARRACKS

SITE OF EASTERN ENTRANCE TO BARRACKS

155mm GUN TURRET

block. Only the eastern ramp exists today.

The shell torn bank of earth that you see ahead of you is all that is left of the inner wall of the southern (or gorge) ditch. On this side of the fort, the outer wall has completely disappeared.

The tunnel that you see today is the only remaining part of the blockhouse that originally guarded the main entrance to Fort Douaumont. The blockhouse, which was set in the middle of a long wall, was shaped like a very shallow letter 'm'. It was composed of ten rooms, or casemates, that were armed for ditch defence. They were protected by an additional ditch that ran the length of the blockhouse and was crossed by a drawbridge. On each side of the gateway, four casemates covered the entrance with direct fire, while further

Ruined entrance blockhouse.

casemates set almost at right angles to them provided flanking fire to defend the drawbridge and the ditch. The casemates communicated with each other internally and the blockhouse was connected to the barracks by an underground passage.

The original gateway was made of dressed stone, with the name 'Douaumont' over the top. The gate was a simple iron door topped by a line of stout railings. The German 'shooting match' of February 1915 damaged the gateway but no attempt was made to clear and repair it. During the battle for the fort, the entrance blocked up entirely and the wagon tunnel partly collapsed. They were only cleared in 1917. Until then, troop access to the main block from this side of the fort was only possible by finding a hole in the huge heap of rubble in front of the barracks, or by using an underground access tunnel made by the Germans.

The damage suffered by the blockhouse during 1916 is so great that it is impossible to gain any clear idea of the size or strength of the original entrance to Fort Douaumont. A visit to the *Entrée de Guerre* at Fort Souville will help visitors gain some idea of its pre-war appearance, although the entrance to Fort Douaumont was both bigger and stronger. The *Entrée de Guerre* is signposted on the dirt track named the *Chemin de Souville*, which runs along the south side of Fort Souville between the D112 and the D913.

The ditch – 2

The ditch is accessible but the path is uneven and care should be exercised to avoid picket posts, wire and other debris Visitors who do not wish to walk the ditch should take the ramp up to the fort and rejoin the tour by the visitor entrance **(8)**.

The tour of the ditch begins on the southwestern side of the fort. At the foot of the ramp that leads to the barracks, turn left along the base of the earth rampart. Although not as deep or as wide as it originally was, the ditch is still impressive. In 1916, the outer wall (or counterscarp) was approximately six metres high. It was faced with dressed stone, almost all of which has disappeared. The inner wall, or scarp, was a sloping rampart of earth. Along the top of the counterscarp, the stout iron railing that formed an additional obstacle to attackers has been completely blasted away but visitors will still be able to see occasional short sections of the defensive railing formerly implanted along the base of the scarp. The floor of the ditch was originally flat and the southeastern and southwestern corners were protected by additional drop ditches that have disappeared. Similar drop ditches protected access to the counterscarp galleries.

It was through breaches in the counterscarp in this section of the ditch that troops from the 2nd Battalion of the French 129th Infantry Regiment, accompanied by pioneers, first reached the fort on 22 May 1916.

Follow the ditch along the south side of the fort to the corner and turn right. You are now in the western ditch. The northwestern counterscarp gallery is ahead of you at the far end of the ditch. The Bourges Casemate is situated at the top of the earth rampart to the right, but is out of sight.

The counterscarp galleries

The counterscarp galleries were designed to sweep with enfilading fire any enemy who managed to penetrate into the ditch. Before 1916 they were accessible from both the ditch and the barracks. After capturing Fort Douaumont in February 1916, the Germans equipped the galleries with machine guns and protected the facades with thick barricades of sandbags. After the French retook the fort, steps were taken to render the counterscarp galleries capable of independent resistance. Each gallery was protected by a wide field of wire and they were supplied with machine guns and light trench mortars. They were also provided with their own electricity generators and independent means of communication. Rations and supplies of every kind were stored in waterproof packing and the commanders were chosen from among the most competent NCOs. French troops were forbidden to use these galleries as a means of access to the barracks or the ditch.

The northwestern counterscarp gallery – 3

Continue along the western ditch towards the northwestern counterscarp gallery, which is at the far end. Stand facing the gallery. You are now in the northwestern corner of the ditch. A section of the original counterscarp wall is to be seen immediately to your left. The northwestern machine gun turret and observation post are to be seen at

the top of the earth rampart to your right rear. The double gallery at the northern apex of the ditch is along the ditch to your right.

During the battle the facade of the northwestern gallery was destroyed. After retaking the fort, the French repaired it with masonry and made the present gun embrasures. Inside the gallery, a fifteen-metre deep shaft in the left hand corner led to the new network of deep tunnels constructed by the French during 1917.

There is no longer any external access to this gallery, which, during the German

Scenes like these were a familiar and depressing sight for soldiers as they traversed the battlefield.

The northwestern counterscarp gallery today.

occupation of the fort, served as an exit towards the front lines and was under permanent heavy fire. Companies leaving the fort bunched up inside, waiting for a lull in the shelling before they made a dash for it. Not everyone was successful and the sight of casualties lying so close to the exit was very depressing for the troops inside.

Like the other counterscarp galleries, this position was accessible from the barracks by a tunnel under the ditch. After the French recaptured the fort, military engineers investigated these tunnels and found them to be mainly in good condition, although partially flooded by water seeping through cracks in the roof and walls. Duckboards were installed in the tunnels but as flooding grew worse, rafts became necessary. Pumping failed to solve the problem and it became impossible to use the tunnels until a new drainage system was installed in the fort during 1917.

The double gallery – 4

Now proceed along the ditch towards the northern apex and face the double counterscarp gallery, which is in a very battered state. The original gun embrasures and doors have been blocked up. There is no longer any external access, and the tunnel from the barracks is still subject to flooding at its deepest point. There is no trace of the ramp that the Germans constructed close to this gallery to facilitate the arrival of supplies and the evacuation of wounded. Until this ramp was constructed, troops and supplies arriving at the fort used a rope ladder and an improvised hoist to access the ditch. Casualties were evacuated by the same method. Lieutenant Eugen Radtke, who was seriously wounded on 26 February and lay for a week in the infirmary of the fort, was himself carried up the north wall of the ditch on the back of a stretcher bearer. It was an experience that he remembered with horror.

Now stand with your back to the gallery. The breach in the counterscarp railings that allowed Radtke, Haupt and their men to gain access to the ditch on 25 February was somewhere along the ditch to the right. The 75mm gun turret and observation post are out of sight at

The northern counterscarp gallery today.

the top of the earth rampart in front and the northeastern counterscarp gallery is along the ditch to your left.

The northeastern gallery – 5

Now continue along the ditch to the northeastern gallery, which served as the main means of access to the barracks during the German occupation. On the way you will pass a section of the original ditch railing still standing on the right of the path. The French were well aware of the importance of the northeastern gallery and kept this area of the ditch under heavy fire. As a result, the outer wall of the ditch is lower and more battered than the parts previously seen. The gallery itself is very badly damaged and looks like a shapeless mass of concrete pierced by several small openings. German troops needing to enter the barracks used a ladder to access the ditch at this corner before entering the gallery through the doorway in the facade. This doorway is much smaller today than it was in 1916. Access to the barracks was by a tunnel from the left hand corner of the gallery, which has today completely collapsed. In the right hand corner, however, a deep shaft leads to the new tunnel network constructed by the French after 1916.

As you face the gallery, the northeastern machine gun turret and observation post are at the top of the earth rampart behind you.

Return to front of fort – 6

Continue along the ditch to return to the car park and walk up towards the barracks. The tour proceeds towards the right along the front of the barracks in the direction of the 155mm turret. It then continues around the top of the fort, returning to the front via the Bourges Casemate and the merlon.

Visible on the right as you approach the barracks are the tunnel from the main entrance, and the eastern wagon ramp. At the foot of the ramp, the original southern entrance to the lower floor of the barracks is visible but is inaccessible. The footbridge that crossed the gap above the ramp and linked the earth rampart to the narrow area immediately in front of the barracks has also disappeared. That area was known to the French as the *balcon du fort* and it was edged by a strong railing.

The facade – 7

When Fort Douaumont was built, most of the archways in the facade were pierced by two windows and a central doorway. The original appearance is still visible in Barrack Room 31, which is

Defensive blockhouse built into the facade.

immediately to the right of the merlon. The facade originally projected for approximately two and a half metres in front of each archway, thereby offering the windows and doorways some protection from bad weather and shelling. Note the thickness of the layer of special concrete that was applied to the facade in 1887 during the modernization process.

At the end of the battle for the fort, this side of the barracks was buried in earth and debris to a height of three metres. After clearing the debris the French replaced the destroyed facade by a series of small blockhouses that were accessible from inside the barracks. The blockhouses were provided with arms and ammunition and, in some cases, telephones, but they were not proof against gas, so the defenders were expected to use their own breathing equipment. In an attempt to prevent gas from seeping into the barrack rooms, the doors between the blockhouses and the barrack rooms were covered in thick felt.

As you approach the barracks, note the major shell damage to the facade and top of the fort to be seen to the left of the visitor entrance. This was caused by a French 400mm shell that crashed into Barrack Room 33 on 23 October 1916, burying the occupants in rubble.

The visitor entrance – 8

A small plaque placed high on the left of the visitor entrance records, in French and English, the establishment of a branch of the YMCA in Fort Douaumont in February 1918. The inscription reads:

139

In commemoration of the heroic days of the Great War when the sons of France and the sons of America side by side gave their lives for liberty this plaque is placed by the Young Mens' Christian Association of the United States. Here stood one of the 1800 Foyers du Soldat of the Union Franco-Américaine erected with the co-operation of the American YMCA.

The regiments that took part in the successful operation of 24 October 1916 are listed over the entrance. Above the list is the memorial to the RICM inaugurated on 7 August 1932 by M. Albert Lebrun, President of the Republic. The inscription in French reads:

On 24 October 1916 the Régiment Coloniale du Maroc, reinforced by the 43rd Senegalese Battalion and by two companies of Somalis, taking, with admirable élan, the first German trenches, then moving forward under the energetic command of Lieutenant-Colonel Régnier, shattering the successive defences of the enemy over a depth of two kilometres, inscribed a glorious page in its history <u>by seizing Fort Douaumont with an irresistible onslaught</u> and retaining its prize despite the repeated counter attacks of the enemy.

Above the memorial, a further plaque records the part played in the recapture of the fort by the 312th Infantry and the 4th *Régiment Mixte*. It reads as follow:

On 24 October, as the RICM set foot on Fort Douaumont, the 321st Infantry Regiment on its right reached the eastern side of the fort and the 4th Régiment Mixte de Zouaves and Tirailleurs on its left penetrated the western ditch. These three regiments, united in endeavour, today share the honour of seeing inscribed on their colours the glorious name: 'Verdun-Douaumont'.

On the left of the entrance, a plaque records in German and French the interment in two artillery shelters of the remains of 679 German soldiers killed in the explosion of 8 May 1916.

From the visitor entrance, follow the walkway to the right towards the 155mm gun turret which is just beyond the end of the barracks. Immediately beyond the visitor entrance are the remains of the *masque de facade* **(9)**. This was a long stone archway protected by a huge rampart of earth, which covered the facade of the barracks between Rooms 39 and 42. The archway was originally designed to provide protection for a type of signalling station that was rendered obsolete by the advent of the telephone. Thereafter, a hot water boiler was placed under the archway, directly in line with the entrance to a passage between Barrack Rooms 40 and 41. The external access to this passage has been

ANTI-AIRCRAFT POSITION   1917 BLOCKHOUSE

1917 BLOCKHOUSE

SITE OF EASTERN
ENTRANCE TO BARRACKS

Former eastern entrance and anti-aircraft position.

blocked up but the passage itself is visible from inside the barracks. The masque was destroyed by a German 420mm shell in February 1915, at the same time as the bakery. The enormous hole left by that shell is still to be seen on top of the barracks. Further extensive shell damage is to be seen on the right as you approach the end of the barracks. The former wagon entrance to the eastern end of the barracks has totally disappeared; the site is marked by an anti-aircraft position which is better viewed from the top of the fort. A little way beyond it, a small machine gun post with T-shaped embrasure, added in 1917 to defend the area immediately in front of the barracks, has been constructed on the site of workshops that were damaged by a German 420mm shell.

The 155mm gun turret and observation post – 10

At the end of the barrack block, a repaired concrete bunker houses the 155mm gun turret, which is inaccessible from the outside. A flight of rough steps leads up to the cupola and observation post. Walk up the steps and stand on the left of the cupola with your back to the nearby observation dome. On clear days, the views over the Woëvre Plain in front of you stretch to the 1914 German border, forty kilometres away to the east.

This is the biggest and most powerful of the gun turrets at Fort Douaumont. Known as a 'Galopin' turret after the name of its inventor, it was built in 1908 at a cost of 350,000 francs. Galopin's original model mounted two long barrelled guns. Five of them were installed in Lorraine but their huge size and cost – the twin turret weighed 200 tons and measured five metres in diameter – led to the adoption of a smaller model. This example mounts one short barrelled 155mm gun capable of firing three rounds a minute over a range of 7,500 metres. It is housed in a three-storey concrete unit. The walls – made of two metres of special concrete – are set in a thick stone packing under a heavy slab of reinforced concrete. The turret itself is a steel cylinder almost four metres in diameter, whose two-centimetre thick walls are reinforced by vertical ribs. The massive cupola is thirty centimetres thick. The steel rim that reinforces the edge of the pit is made in segments that fasten together with bolts. Visitors wishing to obtain an idea of the strength of the rim should visit Fort Vaux, where the 75mm gun turret was destroyed during 1916 by explosions occurring inside the fort. The shattered rim, with bolts attached, lies in pieces on top of the fort.

The turret was activated by a vertical movement that raised it into the firing position and lowered it again once the gun had ceased firing. On the lowest floor of the concrete unit, two huge counterweights on horizontal arms worked like levers on a central supporting pillar. The system depended on the balance between the counterweights and the turret. The turret was raised in the following manner: first, on the basis of reports received from observers, the gun was loaded and aimed. Then a system of cranks and gears was operated to raise a small counterweight. This freed the arms, which allowed the main counterweights to sink under their own weight into the pits designed to receive them. The downward movement of the counterweights raised the turret to the firing position and locked it. The small counterweight then returned to its original position. The gun was fired automatically. The force of the recoil was harnessed to unlock the turret, which came down under its own weight. As it did so, it brought up the counterweights and the arms returned to the horizontal. It took four and a half seconds and a team of six men to raise the turret to the firing position, fire a single round and lower the turret again but if necessary the gun could be maintained in the firing position for a period of sustained fire. The system was entirely manual and a plan to electrify it had not been implemented before war broke out.

Throughout the German occupation of Fort Douaumont, this turret served as a signalling station and a troop latrine. Despite being hit several times by heavy calibre shells, the cupola resisted the massive impacts; splash marks and indentations in the steel are the only trace of the terrible battering that it received. To the surprise of the team of specialists sent to repair the turret after the French recaptured the fort, they found that the turret mechanism had not been damaged and that, although damaged outside, the concrete unit was intact inside. The gun itself was in good condition, although the breech had been removed by

WHEELS TO ROTATE
THE TURRET AND
AIM THE GUN

CENTRAL
SUPPORTING
PILLAR

COUNTERWEIGHT
ARM

COUNTERWEIGHT
ARM

CRANKS AND MACHINERY TO
RAISE SMALL COUNTERWEIGHT

The machinery for turning and raising the 155mm turret. Jean-Luc Kaluzko

the Germans. After replacement of the breech, cleaning and greasing, the gun was returned to action on 15 December 1916.

The gun was served by two observation posts. From the adjacent post, the observer communicated with the gun crew by speaking tube. The small steel dome, twenty five centimetres thick, offered 240° vision through three slits that could be closed by shutters. Inside the dome, which was less than one metre wide, the observer worked with maps and binoculars to control and direct artillery fire.

Now stand by the cupola with the car park behind you. The second observation post for this gun **(12)** is the steel dome that is to be seen on top of the extremely battered concrete block to your left front. From there, the observer communicated with this gun turret by telephone. The second observation post originally adjoined Ammunition Bunker VII on the northern side of the *Rue du Rempart*, but the bunker has been entirely destroyed.

The northeastern machine gun turret and observation post – 11

From the 155mm turret, proceed towards the machine gun turret which is directly in front of you above the northeastern corner of the ditch. Each of the machine gun turrets at Fort Douaumont housed two eight millimetre Hotchkiss machine guns that were mounted one above the other and fired alternately to avoid overheating. They were served by a crew of two and, since they were intended for the close defence of the fort, could be turned and aimed very quickly. For night fighting, an automatic aiming system was provided.

This turret is in the firing position and shows the gun embrasures and observation slits. The steel wall and cupola are much lighter than the 155mm gun turret and were not designed to resist heavy shelling. After the French recaptured the fort, the cupola was found to be intact. The steel wall had been pierced in several places and the turret was difficult to turn but the concrete was sound and the neighbouring observation post was intact. The turret was rearmed with two machine guns and, at the same time, adapted for use as an observation post by having the steel wall cut away. During the 1930s, it was replaced by a new, identical, installation that had been manufactured before 1914 but never installed. Since this turret is accessible, the machinery is described in the guided tour of the inside of the fort.

When elements of the 1st Battalion of the RICM reached the superstructure of the fort on 24 October 1916, they found French troops already on the fort. On the extreme left flank of the 133rd Division, a small unit of the 321st Infantry had achieved its objective of seizing the battery and machine gun turret to the east of the fort. In accordance with its orders, the unit now sought to link up with the RICM. Seeing that the colonials had not yet arrived and fearing that the opportunity to seize the fort might be lost, a handful of men crossed the ditch and reached this machine gun turret. They captured a German NCO and, being fired on from a slit in the nearby observation post, they returned fire. When the RICM came up, the infantrymen returned to their original positions outside the ditch. A 'discussion' subsequently arose between the RICM and the 321st over which regiment was entitled to claim the honour of being first on the fort. to avoid any difficulty, General Nivelle, commander of Second Army, wrote a letter in which he stated that 'elements of the 321st Infantry were the first to penetrate the eastern side of Fort Douaumont, capturing or driving away the defenders'. This was inserted into the war diary of the 321st Infantry and, with that, honour was satisfied.

1917 observation post – 13

Stand with your back to the machine gun turret and face the observation dome on the battered reinforced concrete block. Directly ahead of you at the highest point of the fort you will see a large concrete observation post that was built by the French in 1917 on top of Ammunition Bunker VI. Observation services in the fort were commanded from this post which, being not fully shell proof, was demolished several times.

The 75mm gun turret and observation post – 14

Continue towards the 1917 observation post. When you reach it, proceed towards the 75mm gun turret and observation post that you will see on your right front. This turret, which was installed in 1913, is

75mm gun turret in the firing position with two embrasures visible.

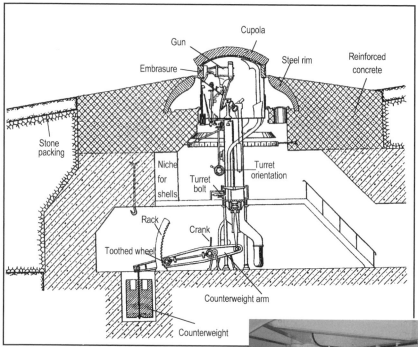

75mm Gun Turret. Bibliotheque Municipale de Verdun Scale 1:1000

not accessible to visitors. Its twin short barrelled guns – capable of firing twenty two rounds a minute over 5,500 metres – covered the more distant approaches to the fort, as well as the sectors on either side. The specifications of the armouring are approximately the same as in the 155mm turret. This type of turret served the French so well during the First World War that a modernized version of it was later adopted for use in the Maginot Line forts.

The turret mechanism was operated manually and required a single counterweight. Two cranks on the counterweight arm caused a

An identical 75mm turret in the Maginot Line fort of Rohrbach-les-Bitche.

toothed wheel to climb down a rack, thereby lowering the counterweight into the pit. The downward movement of the counterweight pushed the turret up into the firing position, where it was bolted. After firing, the bolts were withdrawn and the cranks turned again, bringing the counterweight up and returning the turret to its original position. It took less than six seconds to raise the turret into the firing position and two men were needed on the cranks to bring it down again. The guns were serviced by a team comprising an officer and up to eighteen men.

The cupola and turret wall survived the battering received during the battle, but the steel rim was broken and displaced and the turret mechanism was also damaged. Repairs were carried out, but for the rest of the war the turret never functioned satisfactorily. The damage visible to one of the gun barrels occurred during the Second World War.

The Germans used the guns in this turret in the days immediately following the capture of the fort and briefly in June during the battle for Fleury. Otherwise, although a gun team stood by at all times, the gun barrels were used to concentrate the beams of light from the acetylene signalling lamps that sent messages to a receiving station to the northwest of the fort. Normally the signallers worked in pairs for two hours at a time and messages were sent in code but at times of great emergency, such as the French assault on the fort in May 1916, encoding was dropped. Service in these turrets and observation posts during shelling was an extremely stressful experience, described by one veteran as like being inside a bell when it was ringing.

Stand with your back to the barracks and face directly ahead. The bare rectangular shaped area ahead of you is the modern firing range *(Champ de Tir de la Wavrille)*. The firing range roughly covers the area of the German line of approach to the fort on 21 February 1916. Hill 347, which was taken by the Brandenburgers in the first stage of the advance, is at the end of the cleared area about one and a half kilometres directly ahead of you. Douaumont village is in the forest on your left front. The double counterscarp gallery is visible in the ditch below.

Now stand with your back to the ditch and face the barracks. The northwestern machine gun post and observation post are on your right. Visitors walking directly towards the barracks from this point pass above Artillery Shelters III, IV and V which, although intact, are not open to the public. These shelters stood on the northern side of the *Rue du Rempart*.

Northwestern machine gun turret and observation post - 15

Proceed towards the northwestern machine gun turret. This was known to the Germans as the 'Lotterer turret' after General von Lotterer, Commander of 5 Field Artillery Brigade, who died of wounds received here on 3 March 1916. After the Germans took Fort Douaumont in February 1916, they found a stock of French machine guns in cases. These were set up in this turret and used against the French by – among others – Bernhard von Brandis. He was the younger brother of Cordt von Brandis whose undeserved award of Germany's highest decoration - the *Pour le Mérite* - following the surprise capture of Fort Douaumont on 25 February 1916 caused such an uproar within the ranks of the 24th Brandenburgers. The turret was later used as a radio station by the Germans and was badly damaged during the French artillery preparation for the attack of 22 May 1916. It was finally destroyed on 23 October by a French 400mm shell that also dislodged the nearby observation dome from its concrete bed. In 1917, the turret was repaired and served as an observatory, where its greater diameter allowed the use of optical instruments that could not have been used in the narrow armoured post beside it. During the 1930s, a new steel turret was installed and the dislodged observation dome was replaced by a model brought from Fort Troyon, an unmodernized Séré de Rivières fort on the River Meuse to the south of Verdun.

Stand with your back to the turret and face the observation post. The northwestern counterscarp gallery can be seen in the corner of the ditch below. On clear days it is possible to see from here the American monument at Montfaucon. It appears on the skyline directly in front of you as a low wooded hill topped by a tall, white column.

Rue du Rempart, artillery shelters and bunkers

Remain standing by the machine gun turret. The damaged state of the top of the fort make it impossible today to understand the original layout of the northern side of the barracks. The wagon roads that ran through covered passages at the eastern and western ends of the barracks emerged on the northern side to form a road known as the *Rue du Rempart*. This served the nearby artillery shelters and ammunition bunkers. To get an idea of the position of the *Rue du Rempart*, stand with your back to this machine gun turret and face the 1917 observation post. Imagine a straight line drawn between them. The long depression in the earth to be seen between that imaginary line and the barracks roughly marks the line of the *Rue du Rempart*.

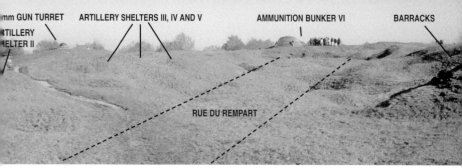

The Rue du Rempart passed through the ridge on which the group is standing.

The position of the artillery shelters and bunkers that used to line the northern side of the *Rue du Rempart* can only be identified with difficulty. Of the two artillery shelters in which the German victims of the explosion of May 1916 were buried, No. I has disappeared and No. II is just identifiable as a shapeless hump under the soil about two thirds of the way between the machine gun turret behind you and the 75mm turret on your left front. Shelters III, IV and V are between the 75mm turret and the imaginary line marking the *Rue du Rempart*. Ammunition Bunker VI is underneath the 1917 observation post. All that is left of Ammunition Bunker VII is the battered concrete block with protruding, twisted reinforcing bars which formed the second observation post for the 155mm turret.

Western entrance to the barracks – 16

From the machine gun turret, follow the path in the direction of the car park. You will have the western end of the barrack block on your left hand and the Bourges Casemate on your right. The path descends towards the front of the barracks. When you reach level ground again, turn to face the way you have just come. The merlon is now on the right, with the Bourges Casemate on the left. Directly in front of you are two recently reconstructed blockhouses. This part of the fort bears little resemblance to

40cm railway line entering the western entrance. Photograph dated 23 February 1917. Mémorial de Verdun

its appearance in 1916. The original western entrance, which was wide and high enough to take wagons, stood roughly on the site of the new blockhouse on the left. Note the recent repairs to the concrete over the new blockhouses that bring out the original layers formed by the 'continuous pour' process used during the modernization of the fort in 1887.

Bourges Casemate - 17

As you face the western end of the barracks, the heavily damaged Bourges Casemate is on your left. Proceed to the front of the casemate, which stands on the southwestern shoulder of the fort. It originally had two chambers armed with quick firing 75mm field guns that were designed to cover the southwestern approaches and to flank the ridge between the fort and the *Ouvrage de Froideterre*. The guns were removed during 1915 and, after capturing the fort, the Germans installed machine guns in their place. During the French assault of May 1916, a machine gun nest established on the top of the Bourges Casemate covered the western entrance to the barracks and pinned the Germans inside. A visit to the top of the casemate makes clear the short distance between the two, and leaves no doubt about the threat that the nest posed.

In October 1916, the southern chamber and observation post were destroyed by a French 400mm shell. During 1917 the northern chamber was rearmed with a field gun, while a light signalling station was installed on the site of the southern chamber. Under the lower floor of the Bourges Casemate, the French excavated a further floor which was linked to the fort by a deep underground tunnel. At the back of the casemate a new blockhouse was constructed which covered the southern side of the fort. The badly damaged roof was strengthened and the new chambers protected by a drop ditch.

The recent reconstruction work does not hide the scars of battle. There is no access to this casemate at Fort Douaumont. At Fort Vaux, however, the two Bourges Casemates are open to visitors and have their guns in place.

The merlon - 18

Return from the Bourges Casemate towards the barrack block and stop in front of the merlon. This is the south-facing extension to the barracks that was added during the modernization process in 1887. The front of the merlon originally featured two archways, each of which was pieced by two windows and a door. Between the archways, a narrow opening marked the end of the internal corridor with, below it, a wide ventilation shaft for the rooms on the lower floor. In the

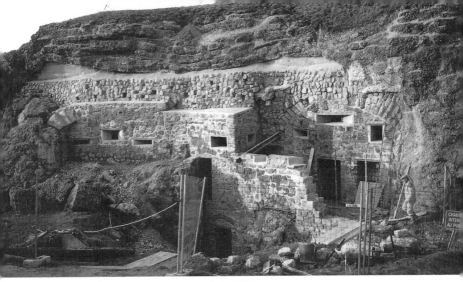

The merlon after reconstruction work in 2001.

immediate aftermath of the terrible explosion of 8 May 1916, this ventilation shaft was used as an escape route from the infirmary. The western wagon ramp ran up from the tunnel on your right, passing in front of the merlon and slightly below it. Around the base of the merlon ran a narrow walkway edged by a strong railing that linked the western entrance with the main front.

Shortly before midday on 23 October 1916 a French 400mm shell struck close to the base of the merlon and exploded. In addition to killing the occupants of the infirmary on the lower floor, the blast seriously damaged the facade. After the fort was recaptured, the damaged southern side was repaired and strengthened by blockhouses with gun embrasures that have recently been reconstructed. The newly restored doorways visible in the middle of the facade were originally made in 1917 to allow access to the blockhouses from inside the merlon.

Stand facing the facade. As part of the general improvement of hygiene in the fort, latrines were built against the outer wall of the merlon on the left hand side. Protected by a reinforced concrete roof and a stone wall, these latrines were never destroyed by shelling. A trace of the installation is to be seen in the slight remains of the roof projecting from the left hand side of the merlon about two metres above ground, and a section of low wall.

The tour of the ditch and superstructure ends at the merlon. Visitors wishing to visit the interior of the fort should now proceed along the barracks to the visitor entrance.

TOUR NO. 3
The interior of Fort Douaumont
Duration – Two hours

NB. The fort is always cool and even in summer it can be very wet underfoot. A sweater and waterproof footwear are recommended and a torch is also useful. While touring the fort, visitors will find it helpful to use the numbered plan of the barrack rooms on page 65, together with the description of their uses on page 64.

It is impossible today to imagine the state of the barracks during the Battle of Verdun. Men who succeeded in passing through the belt of fire that the French laid around the fort threw down their gear with relief when they reached safety inside. They sat or slept where they could, even – as in the 75mm gun turret – on planks laid over stacks of French shells. With thousands of men passing through the fort, dirt, debris and discarded equipment soon filled the corridors and barrack rooms. The walls streamed with humidity. Paraffin lamps used to light the corridors added carbon monoxide to an atmosphere already thick with smoke, dust and gas. With the water cisterns dry, washing was impossible. Sanitary facilities were non-existent and the dead were given impromptu burial inside the barracks. The resulting stench was so fearful that soldiers on both sides claimed to be able to tell when they were close to Fort Douaumont by the smell alone.

The German narrative history of the war, *Schlachten des Weltkrieges*, describes the task of keeping Fort Douaumont acceptably clean as the work of Sisyphus. More than one French commandant described it as a sewer. The empty silence of the barracks today completely belies the filthy and overcrowded conditions known to the Germans during the battle and a considerable effort of imagination is needed to conjure up the conditions that they knew.

The visitor entrance

The tour of the interior of Fort Douaumont begins on the ground floor in Barrack Room 38. This room was used for housing troops until the catastrophic explosion of 8 May 1916, which ignited a stock of hand grenades in the room below and tore out the floor. The gaping hole was not repaired until the 1970s. Until then, a wooden gangway led visitors down the right hand side of the room to the door into Barrack Room 39. The size and shape of this barrack room are typical for the fort but it is unusual in having two doorways into the main

The visitor entrance before the floor was repaired.

corridor. Note the new floor and the extensive signs of damage to the roof. The painting that hangs over the ticket desk shows the main entrance to the fort after the shelling of February 1915.

The main ground floor corridor

From Barrack Room 38 you enter the main ground floor corridor. When the French arrived in this corridor on 24 October 1916, a large section of the roof had been brought down by shelling, blocking access from one side of the barracks to the other. After the French recaptured the fort, they named this corridor the Galerie Mangin, after the commander of the operation that retook Fort Douaumont on 24 October 1916. Note that the roof has been repaired following shell damage.

Turn left and begin the visit in the first room on the left. This is a small museum. After the French recaptured Fort Douaumont this room, served as a chapel. A photograph on the left-hand wall shows Christmas mass being celebrated here in 1916. The partially erased inscription on the right-hand wall reads *S'ensevelir sous les ruines du fort plutôt que de se rendre*: Better to be buried under the ruins of the fort than to surrender. The protective steel plates covering the embrasures in the end wall were added when the facade was rebuilt in 1917. A selection of photos shows wartime damage in the area.

Return to the corridor and turn left. On the right hand side, note the steel ladders that provided access to the lower floor. The plaque on the wall outside Barrack Room 36 records the deaths of seven French soldiers caused by a German 420mm shell on 14 December 1916. A

The celebration of Mass in the chapel. Service Historique de l'Armée de Terre

short distance further on, a passage through two small rooms leads outside. The rusty railings that can be seen behind the gate once ran along the edge of the *balcon du fort*. During the German occupation the first of these two rooms was the telephone exchange.

Opposite the entrance to this passage is the tunnel that leads to Artillery Shelters III, IV and V, as well as to the 75mm gun turret and observation post. A prolongation of the same tunnel leads to the double counterscarp gallery at the northern apex of the fort. None of these sites is accessible to visitors. The operation of the 75mm gun turret is explained in Tour No. 2.

Continue along the main corridor. At the entrance to Barrack Room 33, a plaque on the left commemorates the thirty German soldiers who were killed there on 23 October by a French 400mm shell. This room has never been completely cleared and is smaller than it originally was. The end wall was built after the French retook the fort.

The redoubt

Beyond Barrack Room 33 you enter the 'keep' or redoubt of Fort Douaumont. The roof of this part of the fort, which was known to the French as the *réduit de guerre*, was protected by a concrete carapace two and a half metres thick and it is clear from the state of the original stonework that it was unaffected by the shelling. The redoubt comprised Barrack Rooms 32 to 26, the merlon and the rooms on the lower floor. The ground floor originally provided lodgings for the

154

Defensive walls in the main corridor. Note gun embrasures.

troops, a kitchen and store room. The lower floor provided quarters for the fort's administrative services, the pioneer depot and, if necessary, siege headquarters for the commandant and his staff. The Germans used the lower floor of the redoubt as an infirmary.

Stand in the main corridor with your back to the visitor entrance and face the walls that block the corridor. After the French recaptured the fort in October 1916, steps were taken to increase the defensive capabilities of the redoubt. In the main corridor, strongly built stone walls formed obstacles and gun embrasures allowed for close defence. To prevent grenades from being thrown into the redoubt, strong wire netting filled the space between the walls and the roof. Sandbags were provided for barricades and machine gun emplacements prepared. Steps were also taken to enable the command post and telephone exchange to be rapidly transferred inside the redoubt if it became necessary.

The merlon

Continue along the main corridor. Barrack Room 31 contains beds of a type used in the Verdun forts before and during the First World War. An example of the stoves used to heat the fort is to be seen half way down the room on the right hand side. At the sign for the merlon (*Merlon Sud*), turn left and proceed as far as the first corner. You are now in the east-west corridor that separates the merlon – a two storey extension to the barracks that was added in 1887 – from the original building. In this corridor the masonry archways of the original facade are clearly visible. Note the circular ventilation shafts at the top of the wall and the decorative emblems above the entrances to Rooms 28 and 29.

Now proceed into the corridor that separates the two halves of the merlon. Before 1916, the rooms on the right, Nos. 22 and 23, formed the fort commandant's quarters and the officers' kitchen. On the left, Rooms 24 and 25 comprised officers' quarters and washing facilities.

After the Germans took the fort in February 1916, they used the two end rooms as ammunition depots, but shelling soon destroyed the facade and the ammunition was moved elsewhere. The Germans appear not to have used the merlon for the remaining period of their occupation. After the French retook the fort in October 1917, substantial changes were made in the layout of this sector. The outside wall was rebuilt and provided with blockhouses that were accessed from inside. The supporting wall of brick – to be seen on the left side of the central corridor – was added at this period. Room 24 became a kitchen. A large water cistern was constructed here and a new entrance was made in the north end of the room to give access to a filtering plant in the corridor behind. The concrete workbenches are a later addition, as are the two small rooms surrounded by brick partitions. The end wall of Room 24 is diagonal because the shell damage to the foundations was so great that it could not be rebuilt in the original position. Two doors in this wall gave access to the new blockhouse and the rectangular shaft in the floor provided ventilation for the infirmary below and an emergency escape route.

Forge and workshop

On the other side of the corridor, Rooms 22 and 23 became a forge and workshop. The work undertaken by the French inside Fort Douaumont after its recapture required machines and apparatus that needed maintenance and repair. To this end, a forge, welding set, cement kiln and small foundry were installed in Room 22. A separate rear section of the room contained electrically powered machine tools

Room 24 in the merlon.

such as lathes, drills and milling and grinding machines. Here repairs were carried out and electrical and mechanical equipment produced from recovered battlefield debris. Among other machines produced here was one for straightening or bending rails for the forty centimetre railway line that ran into the fort. In addition to the machine shop, an important woodworking shop produced such necessary material as furniture, planking, timbering for the new underground galleries, stairways, and anti-gas doors.

The western wagon road

After visiting the merlon, return to the main corridor and follow signs to the German cemetery (*Cimetière Allemande*). The last barrack room on the left (*Cuisine*) was used as a kitchen before the Germans captured the fort. Proceed to the junction with the western wagon road and stop.

The wagon road originally passed through the barracks from the south side to the north and provided access to the *Rue du Rempart*. A part of the original surface of the road is still to be seen but there is no longer any external access. At the northern end of the wagon road is the memorial to 679 German soldiers who were killed in the explosion of 8 May 1916. They were buried outside the barracks in two artillery shelters and the site is regarded as an official German war grave. On the left hand wall, a memorial plaque in German and French records their burial. To the left of the plaque is the entrance to the tunnel that leads to the northwestern machine gun turret and counterscarp gallery, both of which are inaccessible to visitors. Latrines for officers and NCOs stood in the wide niche in the wall to the left of this tunnel.

At the southern end of the wagon road, the wall with gun embrasures on either side of a narrow gate was built after the French

The German military cemetery.

recaptured the fort. Beyond the gate a very dilapidated corridor leads to the Bourges Casemate. The heavy wooden planks to be seen there were used by German pioneers to repair and prop up the corridor on many occasions. Each one was brought up to the fort by carrying parties, generally in the dark.

The infirmary

Return to the main corridor and take the first left at the sign reading *Etage Inférieure*, which is opposite the entrance to the merlon. At the top of the stairs, a flight of steps on the left leads to the rooms used by the Germans as an infirmary.

The Germans used these rooms as a first aid post from 25 February 1916 and Lieutenant Eugen Radtke lay there seriously wounded from 26 February until his evacuation on 3 March. Conditions in the first aid post were far from pleasant. The unheated rooms were lit by tallow candles that blew out during shelling, leaving the shivering wounded lying in total darkness on planks and stretchers. With little ventilation, the air was thick with the smells of chloroform, blood and sweat. Care of the seriously wounded was impossible, while evacuation was difficult and cost many lives. In view of the great number of casualties needing treatment, *Stabsartz* Dr. Hallauer, 3rd Sanitätskompanie, III Corps, recommended at the beginning of May 1916 that the primitive dressing station be turned into an infirmary with an operating theatre and facilities for dealing with the seriously wounded. Even so, conditions remained difficult. During the first French attempt to retake the fort, the medical staff were so busy that 'man-high' heaps of blood-soaked clothes, dressings and equipment could not be cleared. A special unit had to be sent in to clean the infirmary and evacuate the wounded once the emergency was over.

On 23 October 1916, a French 400mm shell falling close to the base of the merlon caused a serious fire in these rooms and all the occupants were killed. After regaining control of the fort, the French extinguished the fire. Once the rooms had been cleaned and repaired, they were restored to use as an infirmary. This part of the fort is closed to visitors and for most of the year it is flooded. Flooding is not a recent phenomenon; Lieutenant Radtke referred to the floor as being ankle-deep in water at the end of February 1916.

The water cisterns

From the entrance to the infirmary, follow the stairs down to the lower floor. The French named this corridor the Galerie Montalègre, after the first commandant of the recaptured fort. All the rooms on the right hand side of this floor were originally water cisterns. The cisterns were in two groups, each containing 520 cubic metres of water. Each group was composed of five cisterns that were filled by rainwater draining through pipes from the top of the fort. The walls of the cisterns were plastered and the floor was concrete. Overflow tunnels between the cisterns prevented overfilling.

On the original plans for the fort, the only means of access to these cisterns was by metal ladder from the floor above. Following the decree of August 1915, which downgraded the forts around Verdun and in other parts of France, most of these cisterns became storerooms. It was then that the corridor access was created. By the time the Germans captured the fort, only Cisterns 13 and 18 were used for water storage. There are no records of the German use of the cisterns in the early months of occupation but when the devastating explosion occurred on 8 May 1916, No. 19 formed the pioneer depot and No. 15 housed the regimental staff of the 12th Grenadier Regiment.

The first cistern group

The first cistern group comprises Nos. 10-14. Visitors should begin the tour of this sector of the fort in Cistern 10, which is the first on the right at the bottom of the stairs from the upper floor. Go up the steps into the cistern and stand facing the end wall. On the left there are three overflow tunnels, one of which has been deepened in order to provide access through to the next room. On the right, the tunnel lined with corrugated iron provides access to the infirmary and is a later addition. The insulation still to be seen on part of the roof was probably added after 1917. Once this cistern was dry, the Germans used it for food storage, as did the French after they recaptured the fort.

Return to the corridor and turn right. The next room which is often in darkness and has a very uneven floor, is divided into three parts and comprises Cisterns 11, 12 and 13. Cistern 11 contains washing facilities that may have been installed by the Americans when they occupied the fort after 1945. Note that the metal ladder to the upper floor still contains a remnant of one of the pipes used to fill the cisterns. Cisterns 12 and 13 are inaccessible behind the wall which divides this room but an idea of their layout can be seen further along the corridor in the second cistern group. Cistern 13, which is at the far end of this room, contained water when the Germans took the fort. It was cracked and drained by the explosion of May 1916 but was later repaired by the French.

The next cistern along the corridor is No. 14. This served as a pioneer depot for most of the period of German occupation, but after 1917 it became the power station of the fort. Note that the concrete bases for the generators are cut from the original floor. In 1914 Fort Douaumont was lit by petroleum lamps and had no independent power supply. To remedy this situation, the Germans brought up a number of small generators. These proved insufficient and as a result two more powerful generators were brought up to the fort in pieces. These were being assembled in this cistern on October 1916 when the French recaptured the fort. The German generators were in turn replaced in 1917 by four much larger models (forty horse-power). Sufficient petrol stocks were maintained to drive them for two weeks on full power or for one month on reduced power. At night, any one of these generators was capable of supplying the fort with the energy needed, but during working hours, two or even three generators were in operation. To protect vital areas of the fort, a back-up system of small generators was installed in such important areas as the redoubt, radio station, workshops and the 155mm turret. Damp was such a problem that facilities were installed for drying affected parts of the electrical machinery and two men were constantly employed in keeping the cables dry. The system was controlled from this cistern where a huge control panel – made of marble table tops from the Verdun cafés – could be operated by one man.

The second cistern group

Continue along the corridor towards the second group of cisterns, passing the former southern entrance to the barracks. The tour returns

Cistern No. 14, which became the fort's power station. Note the plastered walls and original access ladder at the far end.

here after visiting the remaining cisterns.

The second cistern group comprises Nos. 15-19. This part of the fort was the site of the explosions and fires that took place in May and October 1916. As a result, these cisterns all show dramatic evidence of serious damage to the roof, walls and floor. A small plaque on the left hand wall of the corridor marks the site of the terrible explosion of a stock of French 155mm shells on 8 May 1916. On either side of the plaque, the wall is scarred and pitted with shell splinters – many of which are still embedded in the stones – and the roof has been repaired.

The first cistern in this group is No. 15. On 8 May 1916, it housed the regimental staff of the 12th Grenadiers, all of whom were killed in the explosion. The Regimental Adjutant, Lieutenant Maron, was found dead at the table. The Orderly Officer, Günther Freiherr von Puttkammer, who was stretched out on the floor, appeared to have stood up and tried to put on his gas mask. The Regimental Commander, Major Schönlein, had been killed on his bed by a stone falling from the ceiling. The regimental history comments that everything in the room was covered with an inch-thick layer of dust and that 'they all looked fossilized, as if they had lain there for a thousand years'. Although the cistern was normally dry, the rescuers found it deep in water that may have flooded through from Cistern 18.

Unlike those that you have seen up to now, the floor in this cistern is of earth. The end walls have been blasted away and rebuilt with brick.

Return to the corridor and turn right. A sign at the entrance to the next cistern room states that it was used as a delousing station (*Salle de Désinfection*). This room, which housed cisterns 16, 17 and 18, has a floor of small pebbles and dirt, possibly as a result of the great heat generated by the disastrous fire in the adjacent Cistern 19 on 23 October 1916. The niches at the base of the walls of Cistern 17 may have served as small fireplaces when the room served as a delousing station. The walls of this cistern were breached after the explosion of 8 May 1916 when an attempt was made to repair Cistern 18, which is at the rear of this room.

Return to the corridor and turn right towards Cistern 19, where the doorway has been blocked up. This cistern played a decisive role in the history of Fort Douaumont on two occasions. After the Germans seized the fort, Cistern 19 served as the principal pioneer depot. In May 1916 it contained a large store of hand grenades and detonators. The disastrous explosion of 8 May ignited the contents of the depot, blowing out the roof and destroying the floor of Barrack Room 38 above (now the entrance). The gaping hole in the floor was not repaired and throughout the period of German occupation this cistern continued to be used for pioneer material. In October 1916 the pioneer depot contained the fort's reserves of machine gun rounds, rockets and petrol. Next to it – separated only by a low door – was a huge store of 7000 hand grenades. On 23 October 1916, a French shell exploded in the pioneer depot in Cistern 19, killing the pioneers who were engaged in moving the contents. The fort's commandant was knocked unconscious and, as a major fire started, panic began to spread. All attempts to extinguish the fire were unsuccessful and, as it was feared that the hand grenades would explode with a repetition of the terrible events of 8 May, the order was given for the Germans to evacuate the fort.

After the French retook the fort on 24 October 1916, the fire in this cistern was extinguished. The room was used to bury the Germans killed during the recapture and the doorway was walled up. At the end of November 1917 the French opened the room again and disinterred the bodies, which by this time were in a state of advanced decomposition. A nauseating stench spread throughout the fort and the French had to use large quantities of disinfectant in order to continue the work. The bodies were taken outside for reburial.

Southern entrance and major excavation work

After visiting these cisterns, retrace your steps along the corridor to the former southern entrance to the barracks. A metal cage covers a thirty-metre shaft that forms the entrance to the network of deep tunnels dug by the French in 1917 and 1918. This extensive system linked the gun turrets, Bourges Casemate and counterscarp galleries with the barrack block. It was accessed by means of spiral staircases that were made in the workshops of the fort. A parallel system of tunnels, twenty metres below the surface, linked the fort's central command post to the 155mm turret, northeastern machine gun turret and the 75mm turret. A shaft dug between the northeastern machine gun turret and the 75mm turret linked the two systems. Additional plans for deep tunnels running for 450 metres from the Bourges Casemate to Combat Shelter No. 2408, and from the fort to the machine gun turret on the ridge to the east, were never implemented. The unfinished German tunnel to Caillette Ravine had already been completed by the French before the deep mining began. This tunnel, which was over 500 metres long, had two branch tunnels leading to additional exits at 180 metres and 300 metres from the fort. Although the mining engineers working in the fort in 1917 considered the Caillette system to be insufficiently deep to offer total protection against shelling, it was not replaced.

The galleries were excavated using electrical and pneumatic tools and by blasting. The debris was used to consolidate the ground outside the fort. As the work progressed, an extremely sophisticated loading and unloading system was devised that was entirely automatic and allowed the evacuation of 25,000 kilograms of debris per hour.

Water and drainage

While in this corridor, note the deep drainage channels that run along each side of the floor. These are part of the drainage system installed by the French during 1917. Before the war, a network of earthenware pipes drained excess water from the lowest points of the fort into ravines some distance away. When this system was destroyed by shelling, the Germans dug drainage pits and installed hand pumps to deal with the water seeping into the barracks through cracks and fissures. These soon proved to be inadequate and the tunnels to the counterscarp galleries became flooded. After the French recaptured the fort, a special unit was set up to deal with this problem and, in addition, to ensure adequate supplies of drinking water. As it was impossible to prevent water from seeping into the barracks, the floors were broken

The original southern entrance to the barracks in 2001. Planks cover the deep shaft leading to the tunnels dug by the French during 1917 and 1918.
Jean-Luc Kaluzko

open and gutters were made to channel the excess water into pits. From the pits it drained to the lower-floor corridor, where the deep channels visible today fed it through wooden pipes into nearby ravines. The flow of water out of the fort could reach six cubic metres per hour. For sudden emergency drainage, a number of mobile petrol-driven pumps were available.

Drinking water was provided by sinking a deep well in the south tunnel and by draining rainwater from the roof. It was filtered over sand and charcoal and stored in vats in two repaired cisterns.

Ventilation

In addition to the original metal air pipes that provided ventilation in Fort Douaumont, the Germans installed a number of powerful electric pumps. After the French recaptured the fort in October 1916, the internal air currents were studied and additional pumps were installed to suck air in or blow it out. By this means the French ensured the circulation of fresh air all over the fort.

In the underground tunnels, ventilation was achieved by the natural movement of air currents. A blower placed at the bottom of the central shaft ensured the movement of air upwards, while another group of blowers placed nearby drew air into the barracks through the southern entrance and blew it through the galleries to the rock face. Blasting was carried out at the end of the day to ensure that the gases had been completely evacuated by the time the next shift arrived.

Protection from gas was a serious problem. To prevent the spread of gas around the fort, every opening was shielded by felt-covered wooden panels, and cracks and fissures were filled in. However, the huge extent of the fort and its battered state meant that it was impossible to prevent gas from seeping in somewhere. As a result, gas masks often had to be worn, particularly when the wind blew from the south where the French batteries were subject to gas shelling. Experiments with over-pressure were unsuccessful because of the vast size of the area to be protected.

The lower powder magazines

Now proceed along the lower corridor towards the staircase at the far end. On your left, at the bottom of the staircase, Rooms 20 and 21 were originally powder magazines. Since no lights were allowed in the magazines, the passage on the right of Room 20 leads to a corridor between the magazines in which lights could be placed behind small windows. During the German occupation, the first room served as a guard room, while the room at the rear was used as the commandant's quarters. After the French retook the fort, Room 21 remained the commandant's quarters.

Communications

Once Fort Douaumont was again in French hands, an extensive and varied communications network was developed that ranged from radio telegraphy to signal rockets and pigeons. The main French telephone exchange was situated in the corridor between the two powder magazines that you have just visited, and the small windows allowed for voice communication with the commandant's quarters. For emergency purposes, a second – smaller – exchange was installed on the lower floor of the merlon.

When the Germans abandoned the fort, they left behind several radio transmitters and receivers. The French added two more sets and transferred the radio station from the destroyed northwestern machine gun turret to the lower floor of the merlon. There were two separate radio networks. A local network served units in the Douaumont sector, as well as spotter and reconnaissance planes. A general network served the forts and the citadel, as well as communicating with Corps, Group and Army headquarters as far away as Bar-le-Duc. In addition to radiotelegraphy, the gun turrets and counterscarp galleries were linked by earth conduction telegraphy to a central station in the merlon. While this system worked well enough inside the fort, attempts to communicate with Forts Vaux and Souville by earth conduction telegraphy were unsuccessful.

Communication with other forts was, however, possible by light signalling. A station in the Bourges Casemate communicated with several forts on the Right Bank and, in clear weather, with those on the Left Bank. A second station - known as the catacombs from its position under the concrete carapace close to the 155mm turret – communicated with Forts Vaux and Moulainville and the French batteries in Caillette Ravine. Unlike the German signalling lamps in the 75mm turret, which burned acetylene, the French lamps were electric and could be manipulated in place or from the observation posts. The receiving station was in Ammunition Bunker VII.

The constant bombardment of Fort Douaumont made maintenance of the communication system, and in particular of the telephone lines outside the fort, very dangerous and resulted in extremely high losses among the troops involved in their repair.

Return to the ground floor – the upper powder magazines

Return to the staircase by the lower powder magazines and proceed up the stairs to the ground floor. On the left at the top of the staircase is a second group of three magazines. When you reach the top of the stairs, turn towards the wall behind you to visit the first magazine in this group (Room 53). The two carvings on the left of the entrance to Room 53 were done by Herr Josef Zink, who was a prisoner of war in Fort Douaumont from 1945 to 1946, when the fort was under American control.

Now return to the head of the staircase. Until recently it was possible to take the corridor on your left to visit the rear magazines but unfortunately access to this section of the fort, which included a short stretch of the *Rue du Rempart* and the entrances to Ammunition Bunkers VI and VII, has recently been lost.

Continue along the corridor directly in front to you towards the 155mm gun turret (*Tourelle Galopin 155mm*). Proceed along this corridor to the end and stop. You have now reached the eastern wagon road. The wagon road originally passed through the barracks from south to north and provided access to the *Rue du Rempart,* which is on your left. On your right, shelling has destroyed the original access to the barracks from the south side of the fort and the wall has been blocked up. The flooring of the eastern wagon road is original. One of the original circular ventilation shafts is to be seen in the centre of the roof.

Northeastern machine gun turret

Cross the wagon road and proceed along the corridor in front of you. The two small rooms on the right (Nos. 55 and 56) were used after 1917 to store petrol for the fort's generators. The repaired corridor that runs from the corner of this room to an iron grille leads to the

Head of Jesus by upper powder magazines.
Jean-Luc Kaluzko

northeastern machine gun turret before passing under the ditch to the northeastern counterscarp gallery. Both are inaccessible.

Twenty-nine rotating machine gun turrets of this type were installed at Verdun before 1914. They were raised and lowered by means of a counterweight attached to chains. A ladder gave access to the upper chamber. To turn the cupola and the gun, the gunner climbed onto the circular platform below the guns, leant back into a specially designed brace and pushed with his feet against a wooden platform. Ammunition was stored in the wall niches on the ground floor of the turret or in further niches under the circular platform.

From Room 56 follow the signs to the 155mm gun turret (*Tourelle de 155*). There were latrines in Room 46 before 1914, although the present installation dates from the improvements in comfort and hygiene made after 1917. In the aftermath of the French recapture of Fort Douaumont in October 1916, temporary latrines were built on the ground floor at each end of the main barrack block. During periods of calm, the latrine cans, known as 'tinettes' – of which you see an example – were emptied in the ditch and the contents soaked with antiseptic. Subsequently, this room was cleared out and repaired and the cesspits were emptied – a task described in the official report as 'extremely arduous'. These latrines were only to be used at times of absolute necessity when it was too dangerous to go outside. At other times, the men used the group of external latrines that were built against the western wall of the merlon.

Continue through this room towards the 155mm gun turret. This area of the fort was extremely badly damaged by shelling during 1916 and much rebuilding is visible. The turret underwent further refurbishment during the 1930s during the building of the Maginot Line of forts. The observation post is on the left of the access corridor, which also houses magazines, workshops for the preparation of the bagged charges, and storage facilities for fuses and detonators. The pit dug in the floor of the inaccessible room immediately on the right of the gun room is part of the new network of underground tunnels dug by the French after 1917. The turret machinery is mostly intact, the ladders to the higher floors have been removed. A spare gun barrel is to be seen on the right of the entrance.

The operation of this turret is explained in Tour No. 2. It required a team comprising an officer and eighteen to twenty men. Although

Machine gun turret. Bibliotheque Municipale de Verdun. 1:1000

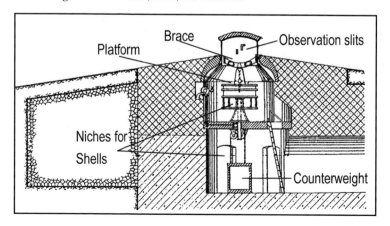

the turret mechanism was extremely advanced, the noise level and the poor ventilation made working conditions very difficult and, in practice, limited the rate of fire. A double hoist carried the shells up to the gun and a hand pump removed the exhaust gases after firing. This gun turret is no longer in working order but an identical one, fully restored, can be seen at Fort Uxegney, near Epinal.

Now return towards the main barrack block. Proceed through Room 46 following signs to the exit (*Sortie*). The first two rooms on the left, Nos. 45 and 44, were destroyed by a German 420mm shell and are smaller than they originally were. A small wooden door in the end wall of Room 45 allowed access to the machine gun post with T-shaped

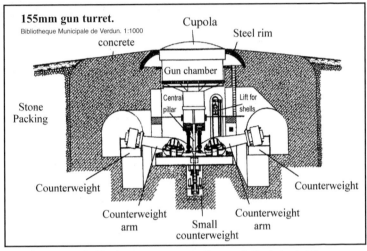

155mm gun turret.
Bibliotheque Municipale de Verdun. 1:1000

The grandson of a Verdun veteran turns the crank that started the process of raising the turret.

Typical barrack room.

embrasure that can be seen from outside the barracks. In Room 44, a hole in the roof enables visitors to see the thickness of the original masonry structure, with the concrete carapace above. The sand has been removed to make cement for the building and repair work inside the fort after 1917. The author has been unable to determine whether this hole also served as access to the 'catacomb' signalling and rocket station referred to in the tour in the section on 'Communications'.

From Room 44, proceed towards the exit (*Sortie*). When you cross the eastern wagon road, take the left hand corridor. You now enter an area of the fort that has been severely damaged by shelling, as is clear from repairs to the roof and walls. The bakery (Room 41), which was destroyed by a German 420mm shell in February 1915, is only half its original length. An opening in the right hand side of the new wall allows a glimpse of the debris left behind after the battle. The passage beyond the bakery originally ended under the *masque de facade* but the exit has been blocked up. A section of the 40cm gauge railway line and a tipping wagon of the type used in the major excavation work are to be seen here. In Barrack Room 40, visitors will gain a good idea of the original appearance of the barrack rooms. Grooves around the windows show the emplacement of shutters. The open doorway allows access to one of the blockhouses constructed after 1917. Further evidence of roof damage is to be seen between Rooms 40 and 39. Continue along the corridor to the exit, close to which is the barrel of a 75mm turret gun. The tour ends at the visitor entrance in Barrack Room 38.

TOUR NO. 4
A car tour of the general area
Driving time without stops – Three hours
Distance – approximately 110 kilometres

Important Note: This car tour does not include Douaumont village and Fort Douaumont, which are covered in Tours Nos. 1, 2 and 3. It leads visitors across the northern sector of the battlefield in an area close to the present-day firing range. On the IGN maps, this area is marked as a long rectangle to the north of Fort Douaumont and is named as the *Champ de Tir de la Wavrille*. On IGN map 3112 ET, the

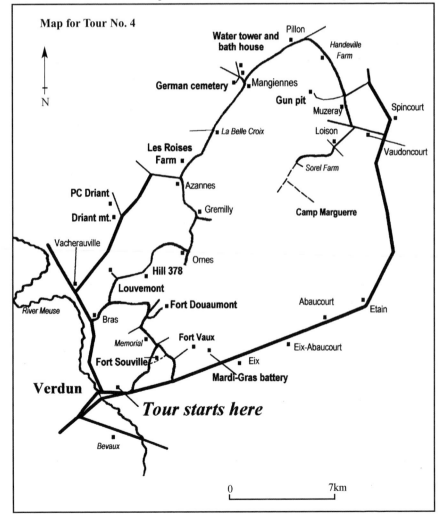

Map for Tour No. 4

N

Pillon
Water tower and bath house
Handeville Farm
German cemetery
Mangiennes
Gun pit
Muzeray
Spincourt
La Belle Croix
Loison
Les Roises Farm
Vaudoncourt
Sorel Farm
PC Driant
Azannes
Driant mt.
Gremilly
Camp Marguerre
Vacherauville
Ornes
Hill 378
Louvemont
Abaucourt
Etain
River Meuse
Bras
Fort Douaumont
Memorial
Fort Vaux
Eix-Abaucourt
Fort Souville
Eix
Verdun
Mardi-Gras battery

Tour starts here

Bevaux

0   7km

rectangle is delineated by a darker green border. As the road close to the firing range is prohibited on Mondays and Tuesdays when the range is in use, an alternative route is suggested below for those wishing to take this tour on either of those days. Visitors should note that there are few cafes and restaurants along the route and it may be easier to plan for a picnic than to rely on buying a meal. Those preferring a restaurant will find possibilities in Bras-sur-Meuse, Vacherauville, Mangiennes, Pillon and Etain.

Yellow Series Michelin maps Nos. 57 or 241 are probably the best for this tour as they cover the whole area. If you wish to use the IGN maps, you will need Blue Series Nos. 3212 *Ouest*, 3211 *Ouest*, 3211 *Est* and 3212 *Est*. The special IGN map 3112 ET, named *Fôrets de Verdun et du Mort-Homme: Champs de Bataille de Verdun,* only covers a part of this tour.

The tour begins in Verdun at the Faubourg Pavé military cemetery on the D603 *(Avenue d'Etain)* (NB: on the IGN maps, this road is still numbered N3). Six field guns stand close to the entrance. Inside the cemetery the central cross is surrounded by the graves of seven unidentified French soldiers taken from different sectors of the Western Front. The body of an eighth soldier, selected to lie under the Arc de Triomphe, was transported from Verdun for Paris by train on 10 November 1920. A plaque on the station wall records the event.

Coming out of the cemetery, turn left. After 50 metres turn left again into the *Rue de Fleury*, following the sign for Douaumont. After 250 metres, cross the *Avenue du 30e Corps* and take the D112, still following the same sign. The road climbs steeply, offering excellent views of Verdun and the surrounding countryside. This hillside, the *Côte St. Michel*, is the last of the defensive cross-ridges before Verdun. When you reach the forest at the top of the hill, Fort St. Michel is along the ridge to the left, with Fort Belleville a couple of kilometres beyond. These were two of the 'panic forts' of 1875.

Continue along the road, passing a small group of grave markers on the right. These recently restored stones come from the military cemetery at the former Marceau Barracks, a sizeable complex of buildings, now ruined, which stood a few hundred metres from the road. The damaged water tank to be seen a short distance further on originally served the barracks. Continue past the picnic area to the monument to André Maginot, which stands on the right. It represents the wounded Maginot being carried on a rifle from the site of the ambush into which his group fell in November 1914. Two simple monuments to be seen a little further on mark the site of the command post used by General Chrétien, commander of XXX Corps, at the start of the Battle of Verdun and commemorate the last-ditch defence of Fort Souville organized by Lieutenant Dupuy on 12 July 1916. Continue to the crossroads with the D913 passing, on the right, a sign to Fort Souville. The lion monument on the right of the crossroads was raised by the 130th Division association and marks the furthest point of the German advance in 1916. The road that you have just travelled from the Faubourg Pavé to this corner was rebuilt by the French in October 1916 in preparation for the operation to recapture Fort Douaumont.

At the crossroads, turn left on the D913, still following signs to Douaumont. The road passes the *Memorial de Verdun*, which was inaugurated in 1967. The Memorial, which is marked on the IGN maps as the Memorial de Fleury, stands on the former site of Fleury station, which served a light railway known as the *Tacot*. Before the First World War, this line ran from Verdun to Montmédy, an old fortified town close to the Belgian border. Continue along the D913 passing on the left the site of the village of Fleury, one of the nine villages destroyed during the Battle of Verdun and never rebuilt. The careful tending of this site brings out clearly the destruction to the terrain caused by the months of shelling, which is even more striking in winter when the shell holes are full of water. General Ancelin, 214 Brigade, who was killed outside his command post at Fleury at 11am on the morning of 24 October 1916, is buried in the cemetery in front of the Ossuary. His grave is to be found at the bottom of the steps that lead down to the cemetery from the road in front of the Ossuary.

Continue along the D913 to the next crossroads. In 1916, the two ammunition depots (*dépôts intermédiaires*) in the Douaumont sector were served by a light railway that ran along the right hand side of this road. There is no trace of the railway today. The jump-off positions used by the *Régiment d'Infanterie Colonial du Maroc* (RICM) for the attack on Fort Douaumont on 24 October 1916 were in the woods on the left of the road as you approach the crossroads. At that time, however, there was no forest between Fleury village and the Thiaumont *ouvrage*.

At the crossroads, the D913 turns right. Continue along the road, following signs to Fort Douaumont. On your left are the French national cemetery and the Ossuary; on your right is *Abri 320*. These features are described in Tour No. 1. Drive past the Islamic Memorial and continue towards the Trench of Bayonets (*Tranchée des Baïonnettes*) and Bras-sur-Meuse, passing the *Abri des Pélérins* cafe, which is on the right hand side at the top of the hill. The war memorial to the men of Douaumont who were killed in WWI stands close to the café and, on the other side of the road, a small monument a short distance away commemorates the 44th Territorial Infantry regiment, part of which formed the garrison of Fort Douaumont on mobilization in August 1914. This was the regiment to which André Maginot belonged. The buildings opposite the café stand close to the site of Thiaumont farm.

Drive past the café down the hill and past the Trench of Bayonets. The deep ravine on the left as you drive down is Dame Ravine, which the French soldiers called the *Ravin de la Mort*. At the bottom of the long hill, the road makes a sharp bend to the left. When you reach the bend Haudraumont Quarries, from which came much of the stone used to build Fort Douaumont, are on the hillside immediately in front of you. Joining the bend on the right hand side (forest block 425) is the *Chemin du Helly* that runs along the bottom of Helly Ravine and Couleuvre Ravine. If you wish to stop the car and investigate the ravines, remember that the *Chemin du Helly* leads to the firing range and that access to most of this area is prohibited on Mondays and Tuesdays between 8 am and midnight. If you do not wish to investigate the ravines, continue along the D913 past the picnic site and turn right on the D115 to Louvemont (*Route Forestière de l'Orne*).

Alternative route
When the firing range is in operation the following alternative route should be used:

At the junction with the D115 to Louvemont, stay on the D913 and continue towards Bras-sur-Meuse. Drive through Bras until you reach the D964 and turn right towards Vacherauville. In Vacherauville, take the right hand fork on the D905 towards Damvillers and Colonel Driant's command post (PC Colonel DRIANT). The road winds uphill through the forest for several kilometres passing, on the right, a sign for Beaumont-en-Verdunois, one of the nine villages destroyed in the Battle of

Colonel Driant's command post.

Verdun and never rebuilt. The small memorial at the roadside close to the Beaumont turn marks the starting point of the final victorious French advance in 1918. Continue uphill to the monument to Colonel Driant, which stands on the left at the top of the hill by a bend in the road. There is a car park on the right a short distance beyond the monument. Close by the car park is the junction with the D125, which leads to Flabas and Moirey. Colonel Driant's command post stands on the left of the D125 about one hundred yards beyond this junction. The moss covered machine gun post on the left of the D125 close to the command post is of French construction and covered the nearby roads, both of which were in existence in 1914.

*After visiting the command post, return to the junction and turn left on the D905 towards Ville-devant-Chaumont. A German cemetery is to be seen on the right just before you enter the village. Although there were dressing stations and cemeteries in this area from the start of the Battle of Verdun, most of the 1766 men buried here were brought from cemeteries in other parts of the Verdun front after the war. Lieutenant Jürgen Freiherr von Eynatten, a platoon commander in 8th Company, 24th Brandenburgers, who with Cordt von Brandis entered Fort Douaumont shortly after its capture on 25 February 1916, lies in Block 3, Grave 334. At the T-junction beyond Ville, turn right on the D65 in the direction of Azannes and Longuyon. At the junction with the D66, turn left towards Mangiennes. The main tour continues from this junction. See ** p176*

Continuation of the original tour

The *Route Forestière de l'Orne* is a paved road which leads across the northern sector of the battlefield to the destroyed village of Ornes. At the time of writing it is passable by normal vehicles but drivers are warned that the surface is poor, the potholes are deep and in winter this road is not cleared of snow or salted. As the road rises towards Louvemont, the Ossuary can be seen on the right beyond a succession of ridges that bring out both the difficult nature of the terrain at Verdun and its natural

New chapel on the site of Louvemont church. Descendants of families from the destroyed villages may still be buried in these churchyards. Anna Holstein

defensive capabilities. At the monument to the French 51st Division, which under General Boulangé held back enemy assaults between 21 and 26 February 1916, turn left to visit the site of the destroyed village of Louvemont. It was recaptured by the French on 15 December 1916 but during the operation *Commandant* Nicolay, who had commanded the 8th Battalion of the *Régiment d'Infanterie Coloniale du Maroc* (RICM) in the recapture of Fort Douaumont on 24 October 1916, was seriously wounded. He died of his wounds on 18 December 1916 and is buried in Bevaux military cemetery, Verdun, Grave No. 164. A number of other victims of both the Louvemont offensive of December 1916 and of the offensive of 24 October 1916 are to be seen in Bevaux cemetery close to the grave of *Commandant* Nicolay.

On leaving Louvemont, return to the D115 and turn left in the direction of Ornes. After approximately 1700 metres, most of which is a straight road, you will reach a forest track on the right which marks the junction between forest blocks 402 and 403. Park your car at the entrance to the track. On the left of the road at this point, the former site of Chambrettes Farm, an important logistical and supply centre for the Germans throughout their occupation of Fort Douaumont, is marked by a grove of tall, black pines. There is no remaining trace of the farm.

Walk up the track to the top of the hill on the right of the road (approximately 500 metres). You are now on Hill 378. On the morning of 25 February 1916, the southeastern approaches to this hill were held by a battalion of the French 95th Infantry Regiment. The southwestern approaches – and the area between here and Louvemont – were held by a mixture of troops that included units from the 2nd and 3rd Zouaves. The hill itself had been evacuated by the French and it was taken later in the day by units of the 8th Leibgrenadiers. Continue along the track, which on the special IGN battlefield map is marked *Chemin du Poivre*. After approximately three hundred metres you will reach the junction between forest blocks 408 and 409. This is on the left. Look straight along the path between these two blocks. Fort Douaumont is on the ridge directly ahead of you, with the Ossuary to the right. While the defensive features of the fort are easily visible in winter and spring, the vegetation is so thick in summer that they can be more difficult to locate. To do so, look first at the Ossuary and then let your eye travel along the ridge to the left. In clear weather you will see the outline of the western ditch of the fort, the northwestern machine gun turret and the 75mm turret at the northern apex. In winter and spring, the machine gun turret on the ridge to the east of the fort is also visible in

Ornes church in 1916. H.P. von Müller's Estate

a grove of trees. This is the view of the fort seen by the 12th Grenadiers and 8th Leibgrenadiers on the morning of 25 February 1916 and it became familiar to the many hundreds of German soldiers who made the journey between Chambrettes Farm and Fort Douaumont between February and October 1916.

Ornes church today.

Return to your car and continue towards the destroyed village of Ornes, which in 1914 had a population of just over 700. Small markers along the roadside indicate the names and occupations of the inhabitants. The church of Saint Michael – a sizeable edifice for so small a village – has been partially rebuilt. It was to Ornes that the French garrison of Fort Douaumont was brought after their capture in February 1916. It was also to this village that the badly wounded Lieutenant Radtke was brought on 4 March 1916 after a painful journey from the fort – the ground was so cratered that Radtke compared his journey on the stretcher to being in a boat on a high sea. The damaged church was being used as a dressing station and Radtke spent the night there before being evacuated to Berlin.

From Ornes, turn left on the D24 towards Gremilly and Azannes. During the Battle of Verdun all the woods in this area contained German camps, hospitals, supply depots, batteries and an extensive rail network. At the junction with the D65, turn left. Proceed through Gremilly to Azannes and then continue to the junction with the D66. At the junction, turn right towards Mangiennes.**

** *N.B. Visitors who took the alternative route via Bras will rejoin the main tour at this point.*

One kilometre beyond the junction a German cemetery is to be seen on the left of the road. Just beyond the cemetery, the wooded hillside on the left above the buildings of Les Roises Farm is the site of Camp Elizabeth. One of many German encampments in the area, this camp is slowly being reconstructed using, in addition to photographs and documents, the memories of the many old people in the area who remember it as it was after the end of the First World War.

The camp, which covers the steep northeastern side of a long hill called the *Côte de Romagne*, was divided into working areas, living accommodation and defensive positions. A light railway line at the bottom of the hill supplied a sawmill. Higher up, the living accommodation was divided into separate areas for officers and men. At the top of the hill, the defensive positions included a deep trench dug in 1916 by Russian prisoners of war, a trench mortar position, and an observation post/light signalling station. Great care is being taken to clear and restore the installations, which also include a water supply, telegraph and telephone links, underground living accommodation and latrines. It does much to explain how the war on this front was supported and supplied for so long. The site forms part of an 'open air museum' which is open each year on certain days in May. Travellers who wish to visit Camp Elizabeth will find contact details for the farm in the Useful Addresses section at the back of this book.

One kilometre beyond Les Roises Farm, La Tuilerie Farm was an important supply centre for the German 2nd Division. As you continue towards Mangiennes, note the wood on the right, which was the site of the important German station named Deutsche Eck and an extensive encampment that was shelled by the French in the last few days before the assault on the fort in October 1916. In the wood there are still many traces of the complex railway system in this sector. If you wish to investigate them, park your car by the wayside cross called *La Belle Croix* that stands on the right by the junction with the D19. Avoid the hunting season, which runs from the end of September to the end of February, and at all times of the year wear stout waterproof footwear.

The D19 leads to Romagne-sous-les-Côtes, now a sleepy and unimportant village, but a vital logistics and supply centre throughout the Battle of Verdun.

Proceed towards Mangiennes and take the second turning on the left (D16) into the centre of the village following signs to Villers-les-Mangiennes and the German military cemetery. Drive through the village towards the cemetery, keeping the church on the left. This cemetery, which contains 3,332 individual graves as well as a common grave for a further 358 soldiers, dates from February 1916 and was in use until October 1918. Major Friedrich Schönlein, commander of the 12th Grenadiers, is buried in Block 2 (Grave 699). Next to him in Grave 698 is his adjutant, Lieutenant Günther von Puttkamer. Both men were victims of the catastrophic explosion in Fort Douaumont on 8 May 1916. Major Schönlein's original gravestone lies at the edge of the cemetery area behind Puttkamer's grave. A further victim of the explosion, Lieutenant Gustav Nitze, is buried in Grave 701. Colonel Josef Abel, 15th Bavarian Infantry, who was killed by shell fire on 23 May 1916 while leading his men into the lines at Fort Douaumont to relieve the French assault on the fort, lies in Block 2, Grave No. 565.

After leaving the cemetery, return to the D16. Turn left and drive for about 50 metres and stop where the road forks. An old grey brick building standing by the right fork and now used as a barn, was originally a German bathhouse for troops. It has an unusual two-tier roof for the evacuation of the steam. Visible on the left of the bathhouse behind some trees is a German water tower, now used as a pigeon loft.

Turn round and retrace your steps to the D66 through the centre of Mangiennes keeping the church on your right. At the junction with the D66, turn left towards Pillon (approximately 40km from the start of the tour). One kilometre beyond Pillon, turn right by a restaurant and follow signs to *Site du Canon Allemand de 380mm* and Duzey. After two kilometres you will pass Handeville Farm, which stands alone on the right hand side of the road. Opposite the farm are grassy traces of a station and rail junction built to serve the 380mm gun in the forest behind the farm. From the station, a main line (144 centimetre gauge) ran through the site of farm to the gun pit in the forest on your right. Remember that the site of the station is on private land and that visitors who wish to have a closer look must always obtain prior permission from the farmer.

Continue along the road through open fields to the next crossroads and turn right, following signs to the gun. The impressive site of the German 380mm 'Long Max' naval gun that fired the first shot in the Battle of Verdun is to be seen in the wood just by the car park. The site, which was constructed by Krupp in 1915 and has been preserved since 1924, includes among other features the semi-circular gun pit, the

Former German bath house.

Ammunition bunkers by 380mm gun pit.

probable command shelter and two ammunition bunkers in the form of tunnels measuring eighty metres in length. Explanatory information in three languages is provided on the site.

After visiting the gun site, return to the crossroads and turn right towards Muzeray, following signs to *Camp Marguerre*, a German encampment and experimental concrete production station in Spincourt Forest. Although Camp Marguerre does not feature in the story of Fort Douaumont, it is extremely interesting as evidence of German 5th Army organisation and industry in the rear in support of the front. The road runs through open country to the junction with the D105, where you turn right towards Muzeray. As you drive through Muzeray heading towards the village war memorial the old water tower with a pointed top that comes into view ahead of you is another German construction. In the centre of the village take the left fork towards Loison and keep following signs to the camp. The road continues across open country for several kilometres before reaching the D16. At the D16, turn left towards *Camp Marguerre* and three hundred metres further on, turn right on the C1 towards Loison. The wood that comes into view on your right front is Watlemont Wood. In the northern corner of this wood is the site of another German 380mm gun pit. The rectangular concrete pit with built-in shelter dates from February 1915 and is a much simpler installation than the circular pit you have just seen.

When you reach Loison, drive through the village with the church on the left and turn left at the junction with the D14. After one hundred metres turn right towards *Camp Marguerre* and follow the road into Spincourt Forest. The road runs through open fields for several

Shelters at Camp Marguerre.

kilometres before reaching the forest. On your left as you enter the forest is Sorel Farm, which is the site of the earliest installation of a German 380mm naval gun in this area. The temporary mountings – enormous concrete platforms onto which the guns were bolted – are today completely overgrown and cannot be seen. The 380mm gun that took part in the *Wettschiessen* (shooting match) on 15 February 1915 was mounted on one of these platforms.

Continue into the forest and follow the signs to the camp. Stop in the car park and walk the last 200 metres to the site. *Camp Marguerre*, known locally as the *Village Nègre* and until recently inaccessible by car, was until 1916 an experimental concrete production station. The buildings and shelters on the site are examples of experimentation with different types and strengths of concrete and shuttering. Particularly remarkable are the camp commandant's house with inscribed front and window decoration, four immensely strong shelters and the site of the concrete mixing and batching plant. During 1916 the camp was used for troops involved in operations at Verdun. Clear information in three languages is available on the site. Local people relate that the camp commandant, *Hauptmann* Marguerre, continued to visit the site of his camp until the 1930s.

Having visited the camp, return to your car and retrace your journey through the forest, noting as you do so the concrete buildings, destroyed blockhouses and many other signs of German occupation to be seen here. Although clear enough in winter, these may be hidden by undergrowth in summer.

Throughout the First World War, and particularly during the Battle of Verdun, Spincourt Forest was a hive of activity. In addition to extensive camps, there were gun batteries, ammunition depots, dressing and casualty clearing stations, workshops, sawmills, stables, cafes and everything else needed to sustain life at the front. Nine hundred metres from the car park, a forest track on the left which is barred by a red and white painted pole is an easy stopping place to visit the remaining traces of an officers' bath house. Some twenty five metres into the wood on the right of this track is a small concrete building which stands above the cistern providing water for the baths. Two of these are to be seen a

German bunker close to Spincourt station.

short distance away, although the wooden huts in which they stood have long since disappeared. Having returned to your car, look for the remains of workshops, including a number of concrete bases for machinery, which are to be seen on the right hand side of the road a couple of hundred metres beyond the baths.

Return to Loison and turn left into the main street. At the crossroads in the middle of the village turn right towards the church. Just beyond the church take the left fork and continue out of the village, passing through open fields until you reach the D16, where you turn right by an army surplus depot. In the next village – Vaudoncourt – follow signs to Etain. At the junction with the D618 (NB on the IGN maps, this road is still numbered N18) turn left for Spincourt and drive through the town, passing the church on the right. Continue up the hill and turn right into the Rue de la Gare at the top of the hill just beyond the baker's. At the end of the road, turn left, drive for a further hundred metres and park by the railway line. Stand at the edge of the level crossing and look to the left.

The German railway network in this area was extremely extensive during the First World War and Spincourt was an important station, as is clear from the enormous length of the platform (500 metres). This station played a key role in the supply of the 380mm gun position that you have just visited and it was particularly active during 1916. Close to the road at the far side of the level crossing, remains of a defensive position are to be seen on the right, with another well preserved two-room bunker in a clump of trees nearby.

Now return to the D618 and turn left towards Verdun. At the junction with the D106 turn left towards Eton to see an interesting example of international aid in post-war reconstruction. In Eton, drive along the main street (*Grande Rue*) and turn right by the church into the *Rue du Bois*. Follow the road round to the impressive *Mairie*, which was rebuilt with the aid of money raised by Eton College, the famous boys' school founded in England in 1440 by King Henry VI. The school's coat of arms and the motto, *Floreat Etona*, are to be seen on the front of the building. Then return to the D618 and turn left towards Etain and Verdun.

Searchlight shelter.

Etain was destroyed in fighting in the third week of the war as the Germans were pressing down towards Verdun. As you enter the town, note a small pink building on the left of the road by the entrance to the Intermarché supermarket, which records the names of eighteen local men who were shot by the Germans as spies in September 1914. Continue through the centre of Etain, where there are several restaurants and cafes. Note that on leaving Etain, the D618 changes its number to the D603. Continue towards Verdun passing through the small villages of Abaucourt and Eix-Abaucourt. After the village of Eix, which is to the left of the D603, the road rises onto the battlefield once again and approximately two kilometres beyond the village a sign on the right indicates the Mardi Gras Battery (*Batterie du Mardi Gras*). Park your car by the sign and walk up the track. Visitors interested in gaining an impression of the multitude of defensive installations at Verdun before 1914 will find signposted here – within a small area – a battery, a rare example of a searchlight shelter and an infantry entrenchment. In addition, a well preserved combat shelter will give an idea of the original appearance of the extremely ruined combat shelters to be seen in the Douaumont sector.

Return to your car and continue towards Verdun. After approximately two and a half kilometres, turn right onto the D913 following signs to Forts Douaumont and Vaux. After approximately two kilometres, turn right towards Fort Vaux by the *Batterie du Tunnel* and picnic area. This fort is open to the public. From the top of the fort, the view towards Fort Douaumont and the Ossuary brings out the great strength of the Douaumont-Froideterre ridge, as well as its dominating position in the sector. The two Bourges Casemates, which are in good condition and still have guns in place, give a good idea of the original size and shape of the casemate at Fort Douaumont. On the top of the fort, the massive steel rim that surrounded the 75mm gun turret lies in pieces whose impressive size enables visitors to appreciate the enormous strength of

The Bussière gun turret today.

such a position. The cupola was blown out by the Germans in the early hours of 2 November 1916, before the fort was finally evacuated.

Return to the T-junction by the picnic area and turn right onto the D913. After approximately one kilometre you will pass on the right the site of the partly cleared Hospital Battery (*Batterie de l'Hôpital*) built in 1881. Approximately one kilometre further on, a sign on the left indicates Fort Souville (*Massif Fortifié de Souville*). It is possible to drive up to the fort, although after wet weather the track can be muddy. Clearly signposted are the wartime entrance (*Entrée de Guerre*), the ammunition depot for the Souville sector (*Dépôt Intermédiare*), ammunition storage niches, and the Bussière gun turret which stands approximately 150 metres from the fort.

Fort Souville, a masonry fort built between 1875 and 1877 and partially modernized in 1888, was very heavily shelled during the Battle of Verdun. **It is in an extremely dangerous state and visitors should observe the signs prohibiting entry.** During the Battle of Verdun, Fort Souville served – as did Fort Douaumont for the Germans – as a front line supply depot, shelter and first aid post, as well as housing regimental and divisional headquarters. During the successful operation to retake Fort Douaumont on 24 October 1916, Fort Souville was the headquarters of the 133rd Division commanded by General Passaga.

The Bussière gun turret – named for its designer, Commandant Bussière – was built between 1890 and 1891. It housed two long-barrelled 155mm guns under a revolving retractable turret that was raised and lowered by steam power. Although the guns were active in the early days of the Battle of Verdun, the turret mechanism proved delicate and soon needed repair. However, the only firm able to maintain it was based in Lille and the German occupation of that city meant that the necessary spare parts could not be obtained. In March 1917 the boiler, which was slow, complicated and smoky, was replaced by a 12hp electric engine. While the guns were out of action, this turret served as a front line command post. General Mangin was based here during both the unsuccessful attempt to retake Fort Douaumont in May 1916 and the successful operation of October 1916.

After visiting the Souville sector, continue along the track until you reach the D112, where you turn left to return to Verdun.

Select bibliography

French sources
On Fort Douaumont

Monographie du Fort de Douaumont, contained in *Verdun et ses forts pendant la guerre*, General G. Benoit, 1929, (Archives du Memorial de Verdun)

Etat du Fort de Douaumont à la date du 26 Octobre 1916, handwritten report by Lieutenant Manhès, (Archives du Memorial de Verdun)

Rapport du Lieutenant-Colonel Benoit au sujet des effets du bombardment sur les fortifications de Verdun, in *Les Armées Françaises dans la Grande Guerre,* Service Historique, Ministère de la Guerre, Tome IV – Vol. 3, Annexes - Volume 1, p. 22 (Paris, Imprimerie Nationale, 1926)

Travaux executés à Douaumont après la reprise du fort, report by Captain Gilson, Revue du Génie Militaire, 1928

Douaumont 24 Octobre 1916, Gaston Gras (Les Editions Lorraines, Frémont, Verdun).

On the Verdun forts

De l'Oppidum à l'Enfouissement: L'Art de la Fortification à Verdun et sur les marches de l'Est (Comité National du Souvenir de Verdun, Memorial de Verdun 1996)

Verdun dans le Système Fortifié Séré de Rivières, Conference paper by Jacques Grasser at the international conference on the Battle of Verdun, 6-8 June 1975 (Memorial de Verdun)

Verdun, Les Forts de la Victoire, Guy Le Hallé (Citédis 1998; ISBN 2-911920-10-4)

La Lorraine fortifiée, Stéphane Gaber (Editions Serpenoise, 1997; ISBN 2-87692-326-2).

On the Battle of Verdun

Les Armées Françaises dans la Grande Guerre, Service Historique, Ministère de la Guerre, Tome IV: Verdun et la Somme, Vols.1, 2 and 3 (Paris, Imprimerie Nationale, 1926)

Verdun 1916, Jacques Péricard (Nouvelle Librairie de France, 1947)

Regimental histories: 129th Infantry, 74th Infantry, 36th Infantry, 34th Infantry, 3rd Génie, Regiment d'Infanterie Coloniale du Maroc.

German sources
On Fort Douaumont

Schlachten des Weltkrieges, Vol. 1: Douaumont, Werner Beumelburg, Verlag Gerhard Stalling, Oldenburg/Berlin, 1925

Douaumont wie es wirklich war, Eugen Radtke (Frundsberg-Verlag)

Die vom Douaumont: Das Ruppiner Regiment 24 im Weltkrieg Cordt von Brandis, (Verlag Tradition Wilhelm Rolf, 1930)

Vor uns der Douaumont Cordt von Brandis (Druffel Verlag)

Seelenkräfte im Kampf um Douaumont Kurt von Klüfer (Verlag Die Brücke, Berlin, 1938).

On the Battle of Verdun

Der Weltkrieg 1914-1918, Vol 10: Die Operationen des Jahres 1916; Vol. 11: Die Kriegführung im Herbst 1916 und im Winter 1916/17 (Reichsarchiv/Kriegsministerium, Berlin, E S Mittler & Sohn, 1938)

Schlachten des Weltkrieges, Vol. 13 - Die Tragödie von Verdun 1916 – I. Teil – Die Deutsche Offensivschlacht, Ludwig Gold, (Oldenburg/Berlin, Verlag Gerhard Stalling, 1926)

Regimental histories: 24th Infantry Regiment, 12th Grenadiers, 8th Leibgrenadiers, 3rd Rheinisches Pionier-Bataillon No. 30.

Specialized terminology
French-English Military Technical Dictionary, Colonel Cornelius de W. Wilcox, War Department Document No. 57, Office of the Chief of Staff, Washington (Government Printing Office, 1917).

Further Reading
These works are suggested in addition to those listed in the Select Bibliography.
On Fort Douaumont
In French
Douaumont: 25 février-25 Octobre 1916, Werner Beumelburg, translated by Lieutenant Colonel L. Koeltz, (Paris, Payot). Long out of print, this is a French translation of the Douaumont volume of *Schlachten des Weltkrieges* referred to in the Select Bibliography
Le Drame de Douaumont, General J. Rouquerol, (Paris, Payot, 1931)
Les forts de Moulainville et de Douaumont sous les 420, Lieutenant R. Ménager, (Paris, Payot, 1936)
Douaumont 1914-1918, Alain Denizot (Librairie Académique Perrin, 1998; ISBN 2.262.01388-8)
In German
Fort Douaumont – der französische Angriff im Mai 1916, Günter Schalich, 1993, produced for the *Interressengemeinschaft für Befestigungsanlagen beider Weltkriege* as *Sonderheft 24*. This excellently researched work deals with the unsuccessful French attempt to retake the fort in May 1916.
Schicksalswende am Douaumont, Werner Lahne (Munich, Verlag Heirich Hoffmann, 1942)

On the Battle of Verdun
In English
The Price of Glory, Alistair Horne (London, Macmillan & Co. Ltd., 1962)
Verdun, Henri Philippe Pétain (London, Elkin Mathews & Marrot, Ltd., 1930)
Education before Verdun, Arnold Zweig (Viking Press Inc. (Penguin) 1995)
The Road to Verdun, Ian Ousby (London, Jonathan Cape, 2002)
Verdun, Georges Blond (London, André Deutsch, 1965)
In French
La Bataille de Verdun, Maréchal Pétain (Paris, Payot, 1929)
Verdun 1916: le point de vue français, Allain Bernède (Le Mans, Editions Cénomane, 2002; ISBN 2 905596 85 6)
Verdun, Jacques-Henri Lefebvre (Paris, Editions du Mémorial)
Combattre à Verdun, vie et souffrance quotidiennes du soldat 1916-1917, Gérard Canini (Presses Universitaires de Nancy, 1988)
In German
Verdun 1916, Hermann Wendt (Berlin, E S Mittler, 1931)
Verdun: die Schlacht und der Mythos, German Werth (Augsburg, Weltbild Verlag, 1990)
Verdun: das Grosse Gericht, P C Ettighoffer (Gütersloh, Bertelsmann, 1936)
Verdun – Souville, Hermann Thimmermann, (Munich, Verlag Knorr & Hirth GmbH, 1936)
General background
German strategy and the Path to Verdun, Robert T. Foley (Cambridge University Press, 2005)
My War Experiences, Crown Prince William of Germany (London, Hurst & Blackett, 1922)
Paths of Glory: the French Army 1914-1918, Anthony Clayton (London, Cassel Military, 2003)
Verdun: ville Militaire, L. Frémont, L. Rodier, P. Gauny, J.-P. Harbulot, G. Domange and A. Bernède, (Verdun, Collection Connaissance de la Meuse, 2000)

Battlefield Guidebooks

There are still few English-language guides to the Battle of Verdun. The Michelin Guide, *Verdun and the Battles for its Possession*, first produced in 1919 and reprinted in 1994 by G H Smith & Sons, Eastingwold, York, England, is interesting but has little detail. *Before Endeavours Fade* by Rose Coombes (After the Battle Publications) also has a limited section on the Verdun battlefield but neither mentions Fort Douaumont in any detail. Verdun and the wider area are covered by Major and Mrs Holt's guide to *The Western Front – South*, published by Pen & Sword Books, UK and by *A historical tour of Verdun* by Jean-Pascal Soudagne and Remi Villagi, published by *Editions Ouest-France* in three languages.

Visitors who read French will find much interesting information about Verdun in *Première Guerre Mondiale des Flandres à l'Alsace*, published by *Editions Casterman* in 1996. Although out of print it is worth looking for a second hand copy of this book, as it covers sites of interest on both sides of the River Meuse and information about the leading personalities. Relevant German publications include the *Militärgeschichtlicher Reiseführer, Verdun*, by Horst Rohde and Robert Ostrovsky (*Verlag E.S.Mittler & Sohn, Hamburg, Berlin, Bonn*) and *Spurensuche bei Verdun: Ein Führer über die Schlachtfelder* by Kurt Fischer and Stephan Klink (*Bonn, Bernard & Graefe Verlag*, 2000). An excellent recent publication which contains an extensive section on Verdun and the surrounding area is *Militärgeschichtlicher Reiseführer zu den Schlachtfeldern des Ersten Weltkrieges: Lothringen und Elsass* by Markus Klauer (2009), ISBN 3-9807648-4-2, www.weltkriegesbuch.de.

Glossary

Counterscarp – The outer wall of the ditch. On the north, east and west sides of Fort Douaumont, the counterscarp was a vertical wall revetted with limestone blocks. On the south side of the fort, the counterscarp was a sloping bank of earth.

Scarp – The inner wall of the ditch. On the north, east and west sides of Fort Douaumont, the scarp was a sloping bank of earth. On the south side of the fort, the scarp was a vertical wall revetted with limestone blocks.

Counterscarp gallery – A strong concrete bunker embedded in the counterscarp in the angle of the ditch and provided with light cannon and machine guns for ditch defence.

Glacis – An area of level, sloping ground outside the ditch and entirely surrounding the fort. It was kept clear of all forms of cover, so as to afford a clear field of fire in all directions.

Gorge – The area of the south ditch surrounding the entrance into the fort.

Caponier – A strong position in the ditch with internal communication into the main work. It was provided with loopholes for the defence of the ditch and the entrance.

Merlon – Normally part of a fortified parapet between two embrasures. At Fort Douaumont the term refers to a south-facing extension to the barracks that was added in 1887 during the modernization procedure.

Ravelin – An independent defensive position, triangular in shape with two sides forming a sharp angle, constructed outside the main ditch and intended to protect the entrance to a fort.

Infantry entrenchment – A rifle pit of masonry or cast concrete, often with a metal shield, which may also have bunkers for shelter.

Casemate – An armoured position for artillery or infantry weapons on a rampart or in a fort.

Useful Addresses

The Verdun tourist offices may be contacted in English

Maison de Tourisme, Address: Place de la Nation, BP 60232, 55106 Verdun Cedex.
Tel. + 33 3 29 86 14 18, fax + 33 3 29 84 22 42
Email: verduntourisme@wanadoo.fr

www.verdun-tourisme.com
Office de Tourisme, Address: Pavillon Japiot, Ave. Général Mangin, 55100 Verdun.
Tel. + 33 3 29 84 55 55, fax + 33 3 29 83 44 23.
Email: tourisme@cc-verdun.fr

Battlefield sites

Please note that opening times may change without warning. At the time of writing visiting times are as follows:

Fort Douaumont

Outside: Any time.
Inside: 1 February – 31 March and 1 October – 30 December from 10 – 1 and 2 – 5.
1 April – 30 June and 1 September – 30 September from 10 – 6.
1 July – 31 August from 10 – 7.
> *Closed mid-December to end of January.*

Fort Vaux

Outside: Any time.
Inside: 1 February – 31 March and 1 October – 19 December from 9.30 – 12 and 2 – 5.
1 April – 30 June and 1 September – 30 September from 9 – 6.
1 July – 31 August from 9 – 6.30.
> *Closed mid-December to end of January.*

Memorial de Verdun (Fleury Memorial museum)

Address : 1, Ave. Du Corps Européen, 55100 Fleury-devant-Douaumont.
Tel. + 33 3 29 84 35 34, fax + 33 3 29 84 45 54.
http://www.memorial-de-verdun.fr/
Spring and summer from 9 – 6.
Autumn and winter from 9 – 12 and 2 – 6.
Closed mid-December to mid-January.

The Ossuary

Address: 55100 Douaumont.
Tel. + 33 3 29 84 54 81, fax + 33 3 29 86 56 54
http://www.verdun-douaumont.com
January – closed, February – open in the afternoon, then April – August from 9 – 6
(weekends) and 10 – 6 (weekdays).

Camp Elizabeth

Address: Les Vieux Métiers, Domaine des Roises, 55150 Azannes, France.
Tel. +33 3 29 85 60 62, fax + 33 3 29 85 62 02.
http://www.vieuxmetiers.com/
contact@vieuxmetiers.com

Verdun city sites
Monument de la Victoire

Place de la Libération, Verdun.

The imposing Victory monument takes the form of a cloaked and helmeted warrior who is thrusting his sword thrust into the ground against the invader.

The crypt under the monument is open daily from approximately 9.30 – 11.30 and from 2 – 6 every day. Entrance is free. In addition to an alphabetical list of all French troops who were awarded the Médaille de Verdun, the crypt houses the first volume of the *Livre d'Or,* which records the names of every French soldier who fought at Verdun. The remainder of the *Livre d'Or* is held in the *Mairie* (Town Hall). Also in the crypt is the first volume of an alphabetical list of all soldiers from Germany, Alsace-Lorraine, Austria, Switzerland, Poland, Denmark, the Czech Republic and Slovakia who are buried in the Department of the Meuse.

Centre Mondial de la Paix (World Peace Centre)

Address: BP 183, 55105 Verdun Cedex, France.
http://www.centremondialpaix.asso.fr/
Tel. + 33 3 29 86 55 00, fax + 33 3 29 86 151 4
The World Peace Centre, which is situated in the former Bishop's Palace next to the Cathedral, houses permanent and temporary exhibitions on the theme of war and peace, liberty and human rights.
Open daily from 9.30 – 12 and 2 – 6.

Citadelle Souterraine

Address: Avenue du 5ème R.A.P., Verdun
Tel. + 33 3 29 86 14 18, fax + 33 3 29 84 22 42
Open December, February and March: 10 – 12 and 2 – 5,
April – June and September: 9 – 6, July-August: 9 – 7,
October – November: 9.30 –12.30 and 2.30 – 5.30.
Closed in January.

Grave location

French soldiers
Secteur des Sépultures de Guerre de la Direction Interdépartementale des Anciens Combattants,
Address: Rue du 19ème BCP, 55100 Verdun, France.
Tel. +33 3 29 86 02 96.

German soldiers
Volksbund Deutsche Kriegsgräberfürsorge,
Address: Werner-Hilpert-Str.2, 34112 Kassel, Germany.
www.volksbund.de
Email: info@volksbund.de

Archives

French archives

Service Historique de la defense

Address: Château de Vincennes, 94306 Vincennes CEDEX, France.
Tel.: +33 1 41 93 43 90
http://www.servicehistorique.sga.defense.gouv.fr/

German archives

Bundesmilitärarchiv

Address: Wiesentalstraße 10, D-79115 Freiburg, Germany.
www.bundesarchiv.de

ACKNOWLEDGMENTS

Without email and the internet, it would not have been so easy to write this book. These days, more and more archives and libraries are accessible online, historical discussion forums turn up information and along the way contacts are acquired and friends made. I must here acknowledge the very great debt that I owe to both old and new friends for the help that I have received in delving into the history of an aspect of the Battle of Verdun whose significance cannot be overestimated.

My thanks are due first to Nigel Cave for inviting me to join the growing list of authors of the *Battleground Europe* series and to Paul Reed for suggesting my name. Secondly, I owe a particular debt to Geoff Mangin, Gene Fax and Burleigh Randolph, who read through the entire manuscript and made many helpful suggestions. Their time and expertise was invaluable and saved me from error on many occasions. Particular thanks are due to Geoff Mangin, who read the drafts many times and whose thoughts and ideas accompanied my research from the beginning.

My initial fear of reading volumes of German Gothic script disappeared as the months went by and I made the acquaintance of historians of the German side of the story of Fort Douaumont, from whom I have learnt a great deal. In particular, I am indebted to Marcus Massing and Jan Carel Broek Roelofs, whose great generosity with books, photos and information has provided me with a wealth of unusual detail, including eye witness accounts of many events inside the fort. It is also through Jan Carel that I have had access to the archive of the late H.P. von Müller – a historical treasure trove if ever there was one.

Many other people helped me. At the Mémorial de Verdun I was assisted in many ways by Isabelle Remy and Antoine Rodriguez. Their knowledge of the archives and their interest in the project greatly facilitated my research, particularly in its early stages. M. Jean-Paul Renaudin of the Bibliothèque Municipal de Verdun kindly provided me with plans of the fort and the gun turrets. At the Service Historique de l'Armée de Terre, Paris, my path was smoothed by Adjudant-Chef Philippe Lafargue who gave up much time to show me around and to help me identify the documents I needed. On my trips to Paris I was fortunate in being able to stay with old friends, M. and Mme. Michel de Briey, who probably never thought that their au pair girl of thirty years ago would turn out to have so deep an interest in concrete and steel. From Seattle Tom Gudmestad sent books and photos and turned up some unusual information, as did my old friend and Verdun guide, Ingrid Ferrand. To my delight, Ingrid was also instrumental in persuading Madame Murièle Sztermer, Director of the Maison de Tourisme at Verdun, to allow me to enter and photograph those parts of the fort that are normally closed to the public. I was accompanied on that exciting occasion by Jean-Luc Kaluzko, whose wonderful photos add so much to this book, and by Rudy Zapp, guide at Fort Douaumont for twenty five years. Photographs of Fort Douaumont and of other aspects of the Battle of Verdun were also supplied by the Mémorial de Verdun, the Service Historique de l'Armée de Terre, Paris, the Bundesarchiv Koblenz, the Imperial War Museum, London, and, in particular, by the Liberty Memorial Museum in Kansas. I was surprised to find that a museum in Missouri would have so many images of Verdun and I am grateful to Doran L. Cart, Curator, for providing them. Every effort has been made to trace the copyright owners of photographs used in this book and the author and publishers apologise for any omissions. Mitchell Yockelson of the National Archives and Records Administration, College Park, Maryland, searched for information concerning American visitors to Fort Douaumont in 1918, despite the very few details that I was able to give him. Martin van Olphen dealt patiently with a number of small but tiresome points concerning the design or original purpose of certain parts of the fort. Len Shurtleff was untiring in providing online definitions of fortification terms from his military technical dictionary. Geoff Stevens drove my planned car tour and checked many details that I had overlooked. My children were a great support. Anna put up gamely with a mother who was suddenly permanently linked to a computer. Isabella provided the first maps and Valdemar was a frequent companion on walks and explorations. When Valdemar was unavailable for walks his place was taken by Jean Poole, whose enthusiastic support for this project has never waivered.

Finally, I owe a particular debt to the extended Randolph family, whose combined engineering knowledge not only supplied answers to many obscure questions but also provided much laughter along the way. In that respect, special mention must be made of Mark Randolph for a surprising discussion, with equations in support, of the ricocheting potential of a 420mm shell that had already travelled approximately six miles. To him, and to all those who assisted me in this project, my grateful thanks are directed. The responsibility for any errors is mine alone.   Luxembourg, February 2002.

INDEX